The Real Estate Brokers Little Black Tax Book

Your Top Secret Guide to Tax Reduction, Business Success and Solving IRS Debt Problems

First Edition
Jared R. Rogers, CPA

This publication is meant to provide competent and reliable information regarding the subject matter covered. However, it is sold with the understanding that the author and publisher are not engaged in rendering legal, financial or other professional advice. Laws and practices often vary from state to state, and as such, the information presented herein is educational in nature, is not individualized, and is not intended to serve as the primary or sole basis for your tax-related decisions.

If legal or expert assistance is required, the services of a professional should be sought. The author and publisher specifically disclaim any liability incurred from the use or application of the contents of this book.

ISBN-13: 979-8610533711

DEDICATION

To all of my friends, family, professional colleagues, and clients. This book is dedicated to you for all of your support, love, dedication, and trust in all that I undertake.

To the two lovely ladies in my life: Aaronita and Pilar. Thank you for all your love and understanding. You both give my life meaning and purpose and help keep me grounded when things get challenging. I love you both now and for all eternity!

CONTENTS

SECTION I: How to Slash Your Tax Bill

INTRODUCTION

Many moons ago, I graduated college with a degree in accounting and returned home during the month of May. I had approximately three months before I started my job in September with the public accounting firm KPMG LLP. But what was more important, as a recent college grad, was the fact that I had one year before I would have to find a place to live. You see, my parents repeatedly told my younger sister and I that we were allowed to live at home after college under one condition: it would only be for a year, and we were to use that time to save our money to "establish" ourselves. After the year was up, we were expected to go and rent a place or buy a home of our own. Essentially, they were telling us "you ain't gotta go home, but you gotta get the heck outta here!"

So, after my year was up, I decided to become a landlord. I bought a place where I could occasionally crash (those in public accounting work a ton of hours) and rent the other units out to tenants. Mind you, I was only 23 years old at the time, so I had a LOT to learn to make this all work. Not only was there the tenant side of the equation, but there was the program side of it (e.g. Section 8 of the Housing Act of 1937) and let us not forget about the taxes. Oh, the taxes! While I had a degree in accounting and had passed the Certified Public Accountant (CPA) exam, I really did not know a lot about how taxes for a rental property worked.

Needless to say, I figured it all out, sold that property some years later, bought another home, sold that one sometime later, and so the saga continues. During the preceding, my wife and I launched the financial services firm Wilson Rogers & Company. With its launch came the challenge of deciding what clients to target. Given that I knew a fair amount about the real estate industry (it was a sector I worked as an auditor at KPMG), it was a natural target to pursue. So, this is why some 15 years after the company's launch, approximately 13 percent of our client portfolio revolves around landlords. If you include clients who are homeowners, brokers, contractors, or investors, that percentage grows to roughly 40 percent.

So why is this relevant to you? I mean, you are a real estate broker - not a landlord. Furthermore, you are not in the tax field. So why should you even be concerned with taxes; is that not what your accountant is for? Well, yes and no. Let me explain.

As a broker, your primary job is marketing. Marketing yourself, your services, your client's properties... you get the idea. Once the marketing is done, you then move on to the sales side of the house. You know, getting the clients to fall in love with the property, dealing with objections, bringing them back to reality, and ultimately getting the parties to sign a contact. Once those two things happen, you then move on to the technical part of your job. That is, the actual part of dealing with the real estate transaction itself and wrangling all the other parties that become involved.

Yet what was not obvious in the three roles mentioned above is this: you are also actually running a business. Furthermore, running a business is not what your pre-licensing class trained you to do. Still further, you were not trained on taxes and how they impact your business or your client's scenario. To that end, it is your accountant's job to help you understand and navigate these items. So, if you are going to select a partner to help you in this area, would it not make sense to find one who is experienced? Given the above, that is where this book and I enter the picture!

My goal for writing this book is three-fold. First, I want to help you understand how taxes impact you both from the standpoint of being a business owner as well as from the perspective of reducing them. It is important for all taxpayers to understand their responsibilities, the associated rules, and what can be done within those rules to legally reduce their tax liability. Second, like CPAs and other tax professionals, brokers are advisors to their clients. The better equipped you are to help your client as it relates to certain tax aspects of their transaction, the more efficiently you can address problems and close deals. Besides who does not like to close more deals? No broker that I am aware of!

Finally, tax problems are commonplace with those who earn money where no income tax withholding occurs. Think of anyone who is paid via cash (or check) or as an independent contractor (i.e. self-employed): dentists, brokers, attorneys, truck drivers, construction contractors, etc. I have known a fair number of brokers who have tax problems. As a CPA authorized to represent taxpayers before the Internal Revenue Service (IRS), I help them solve those issues. Not only do I assist them in resolving their issues, but also those of their clients so that deals can close. The key thing to know is that no matter how bad it initially seems, I have never been unable to help a client solve their tax debt matter.

The knowledge contained within this book has taken me many years to acquire via the tax returns that I have prepared or reviewed and the tax debt cases I have worked. It is my hope that by the end of this book, you will have gained some genuine insight on how to pay the minimum amount of taxes that you are legally obligated to pay (and not a penny more). Additionally, I want you to gain some skills that will help you improve your business operations, client satisfaction, and hopefully lead you to close more deals.

No one really wants to go to sleep at night wondering if they are on the IRS' list of people to contact the next day. So, with that said, let us get started showing you how to slash your taxes, achieve business success, and solve tax debt problems!

SECTION I
How to Slash Your Tax Bill

CHAPTER 1
What Every Broker Wishes They Knew When They Began Their Careers

When you take your real estate pre-licensing class, you learn real estate vocabulary, national and jurisdictional laws, the Code of Ethics... just to name a few. But what they do not teach you in pre-licensing class is what it is actually like to BE a real estate broker. Some of you may be saying, "I am not a broker, Jared. I am just an agent starting out." So, before we get too far into our journey, I want to clarify something. For the purposes of <u>this book</u>, the following designations are defined as such:

- **Broker** - Once you complete your mandatory pre-licensing course and pass the state exam, you can start helping your clients buy and sell properties. Your business card might identify you as a "Real Estate Agent" or "Real Estate Broker" depending on the state you reside in. Here in Illinois, the term "broker" is used. The distinguishing point is that you cannot work on your own or hire other Agents/Brokers to work for you. In fact, you are required to work for a Managing Broker.

- **Managing Broker** - A Managing Broker is a real estate professional who has invested additional time and money into his or her education and passed a Managing Broker exam. Each state has its own requirements for certification training and the exam process. Typically, you need to have a few years of experience as a licensed broker to be allowed to become a Managing Broker. Managing Brokers are able to hire other brokers to work for them.

- **Realtor®** - Often the terms "Realtor®" and "Real Estate Agent" are used interchangeably. Both are licensed professionals who can help clients with their real estate needs. However, a Realtor® is so called if he or she is a member of the National Association of Realtors® (NAR).

So, the term Realtor® is a trademarked name and can only be used by those who are part of the NAR. Members of the NAR are held to a strict code of professional conduct and ethics. You must be a licensed broker to become a member.

So, now that we have that out of the way, let us continue, shall we?

You may wonder why a book about taxes leads off with a whole chapter discussing what experienced brokers wish they knew when they began their businesses. Well, like the saying goes, "you do not know what you do not know." So, since we are on an educational journey, I think it is important to start out on a solid foundation. That foundation does not just include taxes, it also includes understanding some of the "realities" of being in your industry. For, once understood, it will help set you up for success and reduce the chances of encountering financial or tax problems. Capiche?

Being a broker is expensive

You may have heard that becoming a real estate broker is one of the least expensive businesses you can start. While that may be true, it is not necessarily "inexpensive" either. By the time a person has paid for the course, paid to sit for the state exam, joined the local and national board, purchased errors and omission insurance, bought lockbox access, and subscribed to Multiple Listing Service (MLS), the fees begin to add up. In addition to this, you will probably have to shell out for any marketing materials you decide to purchase. It would be nice if they taught this in your classes so you would have known how much money to have saved up!

Yet, while all these costs can catch you off guard, just know that they are needed for you to be successful. The above purchases will enable you to not only start, but eventually grow your business. So, it may be more appropriate to view them as an investment in your future, as opposed to an outright expense.

You do not actually make your own schedule

When I first started working in our business, people would always say things like, "It must be nice to be your own boss. You can pick and choose when you work." I often replied that yes, I had a choice when it came to when I worked. I had 24 hours each day, and I often chose to work them all! Okay, so I jest. When it really comes down to it, it is the clients of the business who determine how much I work. Yet, as an experienced entrepreneur, it is up to me to put boundaries on my time (e.g. office hours) so that I can have a personal life and not work 24/7.

It can be pretty eye-opening to learn that people who work for themselves as real estate brokers work as much as they do. It is true that you can create your own schedule, but the one thing to understand about being a good broker is that although you do not work for one person (a boss), you work for (and want to work with) many people. They are called your clients, and they pay your bills. You could be in the middle of dinner and a client will call you to tell you their world will end if they do not see the home just listed an hour ago. What do you do? Get out the plastic containers and hope your dinner tastes good in a few hours!

Your friends and family might not hire you

When my wife and I started our business back in 2005, most of our clients were exclusively friends and family. Once our retail office opened in 2012, our client base quickly expanded to include members of the general public. Fast forward to now and our client base is approximately 1,200 percent what it was when we were servicing just friends and family. So why the explosion in clients? Probably for the same reason that you will likewise experience in the real estate industry.

Let us face it, when your first start out you are new. In the real estate business, experience matters, and it matters a lot. When you start out, you do not have much of it. So, do not be offended when Uncle Drew, your friend Bubba, or even Mom and Dad go with "their guy" or "their girl" to handle their transactions. Honestly, can you really blame them? There are many ways to handle this, and hopefully someone in your office will teach you how to get past this objection. Why? Well, because as a new broker, you will hear it on almost every listing appointment.

"How many homes have you sold this year?" You can respond truthfully with, "Well, none, but..." That will not probably sit well with your new client. So, it might be better to think of your family and friends as a referral source. They may not use you personally, but they surely want to help you succeed. One thing that also needs to be stated, but is not obvious, is the personal nature of a real estate transaction. It often requires divulging a lot of private financial information to a broker. Quiet as it is kept, your friends and family might not want you to know how much they make or what their loan details are!

Therefore, your job in the beginning is to make sure everyone you know understands what you do and that you are available to assist them. Eventually, someone will take a chance on you, and then you are off to the races!

Being a rock-star broker is harder than you think

Most people have an idea of what a job entails when they study for it in school or apply for their first position. However, when you begin your career as a broker, you might not be so certain on what "exactly" your job is. So, let us clear things up; being a broker is not a career. You are starting a business and becoming an entrepreneur. What is your business? It is not necessarily servicing clients as one may think. It is actually mostly about lead generation.

If you want to be good at this, it will take some work. Want to be great at it? Well, that will consume your life. One of the things I have seen successful brokers do is begin each year with the end in mind. In essence, they:

- determine how much revenue they would like to generate that year,
- based on how much they net (on average) per transaction, they determine how many home sales they must be involved in and finally,
- they determine the number of leads required to hit the sales target.

As you can see from the above, once you have done the math, you STILL need to go out and generate the leads. While an established broker may have a system for this, most who are new to the industry will not. This is where the "rubber meets the road," so to speak, and why being a rock-star broker is so hard. You must cultivate a lot of leads, and do so consistently, in order to hit your sales numbers. Throw in a cyclical economy, differing client personalities, and the ever-looming burnout and you can see how this field is a lot harder than it looks.

It takes time

According to the *2018 National Association of Realtors® Member Profile*, the median gross income Realtors® earned from real estate activities was $39,800 in 2017. Those licensed as sales agents typically reported a median income of $29,440. As you may know, income earned as a broker is typically commensurate with experience. Realtors® with 16 years or more experience had a median gross income of $78,850.

When reviewing additional sources, Payscale.com[1] reports that the average annual income for a broker was a little over

$48,000 in 2019. The Glassdoor[2] page for Keller Williams Real Estate reports an average income of $54,000. Keep in mind that these averages consider brokers with various levels of experience – both those new to the industry and ones who have been at it for a while.

In speaking with many brokers who have been in the industry a while, one piece of advice they often mention being told in the beginning was "do not quit your day job" when starting out. It takes time for you to build a database, market yourself, and generate a consistent flow of leads that eventually turn into commissions. There is no such thing as overnight success in real estate.

There is not a lot I can do to prepare new brokers for the time it takes to get their first clients, let alone build a thriving real estate business, except to break it to them gently. It can take anywhere from three to six months before you get your first client. This does not mean going to closing – this is just the time it takes to get a client. Getting to closing can take another few months, assuming things go well and the deal does not fall apart. With that said, building a business takes planning, time, and consistent effort. To weather the storm until the clouds part and the heavens rejoice, many suggest that new brokers:

- have some savings before they begin and,
- "transition" into life as a broker as opposed to going "all in" without a backup source of income.

Be prepared for the market cycles

If you are relatively new to real estate, you will recall the market downturn of 2008 in response to the Great Recession. If you are more seasoned, you will also recall the downturn of 1992 which also followed a stock market "correction," so to speak. According to financial blogger Philip J. Anderson[3], "For the first 144 years of real estate enclosure in the U.S., land sales and/or real estate construction peaked almost consistently every 18 years. The world's worst downturns are always preceded by land speculation (the chasing of the economic rent) fueled by misguided credit creation courtesy of the banks." So, what does this mean exactly? It means that in real estate, there have always been good times which inevitably are followed by bad times.

Unfortunately, when things are good, humans tend to forget the pain associated with the bad times. In business, this typically manifests itself as reduced attention to marketing and sales, relaxed inquiry surrounding spending, a decreased focus on the bottom line, and of course, diminished rates of saving. Yet, when the predictable downturn occurs, many are not prepared to batten down the hatches until it is safe to surface and continue the mission.

As previously mentioned, it is advisable for a new broker to have some savings. How much? It all depends, but a cash reserve of 2 to 3 months of living expenses is not a bad start. In addition to that nest egg, a new broker also needs to have a "proactive" approach to both their business and personal life. This means scanning the horizon for threats, planning for them, and executing a course of action. If you see an iceberg in the water, you might be able to change course in time to continue to enjoy smooth sailing. But if you wait until the boat is taking on water to address the problem, there is a probability that the ship might sink with you on it!

You will think you made a huge mistake

Sometimes one of your clients will experience buyer's remorse after the seller has accepted their offer. It is completely normal. The same is true for some who become brokers. After attending a few sales meetings and trainings, you may feel like the experienced brokers are speaking a foreign language. You will feel overwhelmed and think you made the biggest mistake of your life by quitting your corporate, steady job with its dependable paycheck for a career that you do not quite understand (yet).

The best thing to do is to keep doing the work. Keep asking questions. Keep attending the meetings and, before you know it, you will be speaking the same language and feeling more confident in your abilities. Any one of us who has ever left the predictability of a paycheck from an employer gets a little overwhelmed once we strike out on our own. It is totally normal. What I often tell people in my field is that you have to get comfortable being uncomfortable. There are many things in this world that we have no control over. So, focus on what you can control, which is your effort to go out and find new leads each and every day. Outside of that, there is no use in worrying about things that may never happen!

Do not give up

It is entirely possible that you will not make anything for the first few months as you just begin acquiring clients. However, with hard work and dedication, that income will undoubtedly go up. Plus, outside of the income, there are many reasons brokers go into this field:

- You get to help people, young and old, move forward in their lives.
- You get to choose how and when you will work (i.e. flexibility).
- Your earning potential is largely tied to how hard you work and your productivity.
- You have the opportunity to build a business that looks and operates how YOU want it to.
- With every completed transaction, you will learn more about yourself, your clients and how to run a business.

I left Corporate America almost 8 years ago as I am writing this. I have had my share of good years. I have also had those years where I wondered why I am still doing this. But like they say, nothing worth having comes easy and being a successful broker is no exception. So, if you are just starting out, or are a seasoned professional who is going through a rough patch, remember to hang in there. Do not give up the fight until you are absolutely forced to, and try to be the best you can be every day.

SUMMARY

- To set yourself up for success and reduce the chances of encountering financial or tax problems, you should obtain a solid foundation in both tax and business operations.
- It costs money to be a broker. But the investment in yourself will prove worthwhile down the road.
- Clients pay your salary. Set boundaries on your time, but realize that you need to be flexible in order to generate the revenue you desire.
- Your friends and family may not use you personally, but they surely want to help you succeed. Therefore, think of them as a referral source and make sure everyone knows that you are striking out on your own.
- Your primary business is that of generating leads, which takes work. If you want to be successful, you must always be developing your database and a pipeline of leads.
- It takes time for the money to start to roll in. Have some savings when you start and plan for things to take a while.
- This industry is cyclical with its ups and downs. Take a proactive approach to your business and life. Always look to plan ahead so that you do not have to react.
- You may think you have made a mistake once you enter the field. This is normal and most people go through it.
- Do not give up. Things can be hard, frustrating, and downright scary at times. But the positives can/do far outweigh the negatives if you just keep at it long enough.

NOTES

[1] PayScale. "Real Estate Agent Salary." Payscale.com. https://www.payscale.com/research/US/Job=Real_Estate_Agent/Salary (Accessed

November 30, 2019).

[2] Glassdoor. "Keller Williams Real Estate Agent Salaries." Glassdoor.com. https://www.glassdoor.com/Salary/Keller-Williams-Real-Estate-Agent-Salaries-E114145_D_KO16,33.htm (Accessed November 30, 2019).

[3] Goldschein,Eric. "The Complete History of US Real Estate Bubbles Since 1800" Businessinsider.com. https://www.businessinsider.com/the-economic-crash-repeated-every-generation-1800-2012-1 (Accessed November 30, 2019).

CHAPTER 2
Maximizing Tax Deductions

Maximizing your tax deductions is not solely about finding things to deduct. While that is a large part of it, also involved is being knowledgeable about what is deductible AND then tracking said deductions. I mean, if you fail to track what you can deduct, then how can you actually deduct it? Sure, you can estimate or even make it up. But guess what? That is a sure-fire way to have the IRS disallow the expense if they decide to audit your return. I will discuss record keeping in the next chapter; but for now, let us focus on what you can write off.

100+ legal tax deductions for real estate brokers
Real estate brokers, who are, by and large, self-employed can usually relate to the importance of tax deductions. By reducing your taxable income, deductions naturally become your best friend during tax time. The problem, though, is determining what can and cannot be deducted. While it is always a best practice to consult your accountant, a cheat sheet sure helps to jog one's memory so things you are entitled to deduct are not overlooked. To that end, here is a list of things to consider tracking and deducting at tax time:

Advertising
- Billboards
- Brochures/Flyers
- Business Cards
- Copy Editor Fees
- Direct Mail
- Email Marketing and Newsletters
- Graphic Designer Fees
- Internet Ads (Google, Facebook, etc.)
- Leads/Mailing Lists
- Marketing Services

- Networking Event Costs
- Post Cards
- Print Ads (Newspapers and Magazines)
- Promotional Materials
- Radio Ads
- Signage/Banners
- Television Ads
- Web Design
- Web Hosting and Domain Fees

Auto Expenses

- Car Washes
- Depreciation/Lease Payments
- Gas
- Insurance
- Interest
- License/Registration
- Maintenance
- Repairs
- Tires

Business Travel

- Airfare
- Car Rental
- Dry Cleaning/Laundry
- Lodging
- Meals
- Parking/Tolls
- Taxi, Train, Subway, Bus
- Tips

Communication

- Answering Services
- Cell Phone Service

- Fax Expenses/eFax
- Interactive Voice Response (IVR)
- Internet Service
- Office Telephone/VOIP
- Pagers (those still exist?)
- Toll Free Number

Equipment
- Briefcase
- Calculator
- Camera/Lenses
- Cellphone/Smartphone
- Cleaning Equipment (Vacuum Cleaner)
- Computer
- Equipment Repair
- Flashlight
- GPS
- Hard Drives/Thumb Drives
- iPad/Tablet PC/Android
- Laptop
- Lock Boxes/Locksmiths/Keys
- Maps
- Printer
- Scanner
- Staging Items – Furniture
- Tape Measure
- Video Camera

Employee Wages
- Clerical Support
- Family Wages (e.g. kids/spouses)
- Payroll/Unemployment Taxes
- Sales Assistant
- Virtual Assistant

Health Insurance, Home Office
- Insurance
- Mortgage Interest/Rent
- Property Taxes
- Repairs/Maintenance
- Security System
- Utilities

Office Expenses
- Desk Fees
- Client Refreshments (Coffee, Water, etc.)
- Copier Fees
- Janitorial Services
- Office Furniture
  - Bookshelves
  - Chairs
  - Desks
  - Filing Cabinets
- Office Supplies
  - Envelopes
  - Folders
  - Paper
  - Pens
  - Postage
  - Stationary
  - Toner/Ink
- Office Rent
- Online Storage of Business Files
- Software

Professional Fees
- Association Dues/Fees
  - NAR
  - CAR
  - NAIREB

- o NAREB
- o NAEBA
- o CREA
- Chamber of Commerce
- Bank Fees
- Bookkeeping Fees
- Business Licenses
- E & O Insurance
- Franchise/Affiliation Fees
- Interest on Business Purchases
- Legal Fees
- MLS Fees
- Tax Prep Fees

Retirement
- Defined Benefit Plan
- Simplified Employee Pension (SEP)
- Simple IRA
- Solo 401k

Selling Expenses
- Appraisal Fees
- CL100 Fees
- Client Gifts (<$25 per client)
- Closing Attorney Fees
- Concessions
- Courier Services/Delivery Fees
- Finder Fees/Referral Fees
- Home Repairs to sell listed property
- Home Warranty
- Inspection Fees
- Notary Fees
- Open House Expenses
- Photo Editing

- Staging Fees

Start Up Expenses
- Including organizational costs

Training & Improvement
- Books (Sales Books, Real Estate Books, etc.)
- Continuing Education
- Magazine Subscriptions
- Newsletter Subscriptions
- Sales Training/Coaching
- Seminars
- Textbooks/Reference Books
- Trade Publications

Author's note: There are certain rules that need to be considered in order to legally write off some of these expenses. As such, make sure that you consult with a tax professional before filing your tax return.

Meals – presentation versus business

Meal expenses for business are a subject that often confuses most people. Furthermore, beginning January 2018, the Tax Cuts and Jobs Act (TCJA) eliminated the tax deduction for entertainment and for food and beverages that are considered "entertainment." Notwithstanding the preceding, taxpayers may generally deduct 50 percent of food and beverage expenses associated with operating their trade or business.[1] For the IRS to consider a business meal allowable, it must meet the following conditions:

1. The expense is an ordinary and necessary expense paid or incurred during the taxable year in carrying on any trade or business[2];
2. The expense is not lavish or extravagant under the circumstances;

3. The taxpayer, or an employee of the taxpayer, is present at the furnishing of the food or beverages;

4. The food and beverages are provided to a current or potential business customer, client, consultant, or similar business contact; and

5. In the case of food and beverages provided during or at an entertainment activity, the food and beverages are purchased separately from the entertainment, or the cost of the food and beverages is stated separately from the cost of the entertainment on one or more bills, invoices, or receipts. The entertainment disallowance rule may not be circumvented through inflating the amount charged for food and beverages.

Author's note: Sometimes clients like to bring me receipts to "prove" the validity of their expense. I actually prefer spreadsheets and will bill clients for having to go through mounds of receipts. But that is a story for another time! Needless to say, if I see a Starbucks or Dunkin Donuts receipt showing a coffee and pastry for 175+ days of the year, I will often exclude the amount(s) from the tax return. Why? Because you cannot legitimately write off your lunch every day when you did not meet with anyone else during those meals (see item 4 above)!

To ensure a meal expense deduction passes IRS scrutiny, I personally often employ an "old school" tactic that works pretty well. On the receipt, I document:

- The names of the parties present
- Where we met (e.g. circle the store address)
- The business purpose of the meal (e.g. potential business customer)

Doing the above typically satisfies the 5 points previously outlined. It also reduces the chances of an IRS Revenue Agent disallowing or removing the expense during an audit.

Presentation Meals

Now what about those donuts, pastries, fruit, and beverages purchased for sales presentations for prospects or your weekly internal sales meeting? The short answer is that they are NOT subject to the 50 percent haircut that other business meals will experience. You are probably saying, "Do tell, Jared." But of course! Generally speaking, meals that are:

- furnished to employees for the convenience of the employer; or
- provided to the general public as a means of advertising or promoting goodwill

are typically considered 100 percent deductible.[3] The key difference with these meals is that they are not for the benefit of the business owner themselves. Meaning, they are not the one primarily deriving value from it.

Retirement plan contributions

One day, down the road, you will want to stop working. Whether that is due to a long successful career, burnout, or declining health, the truth is that no one can work forever. While I feel that everyone should be stashing away at least 10 percent of what they make for retirement, I know that many people do not. But what if I could show you how it could be a win-win proposition for you? Read on, my friend!

You see, the government does not want you to be a burden on society during your golden years. True, they will provide for you if you have worked and contributed to social security. However, do you think that social security will provide you with enough income for you to live the type of retirement you want? Per the Social Security Administration, the average Social Security retirement benefit in October 2019[4] was $1,477 per month or about $17,724 per year. With that said, if you think you will need more than that to retire on, it will be up to you to kick in the difference!

The good news is that the government offers some fairly nice tax incentives for contributing to a retirement plan. These come in the form of tax credits and deductions. While credits are worth more than deductions from a tax perspective, realize that the government allows people to make some fairly sizeable contributions to certain retirement accounts. To that end, they can yield some valuable tax deductions. Thus, if you can set yourself up for the retirement of your dreams AND get a tax deduction for it, why not do it? Hopefully my previous win-win comment now makes more sense.

What follows is a discussion of the retirement accounts most commonly used by brokers.

Traditional IRA
- **Best for:** Those just starting out or saving less than $6,000 a year towards retirement.
- **Contribution limit:** Up to $6,000 in 2020, plus a $1,000 catch-up contribution for those 50 or older.
- **Employee element:** None. These are individual plans. If you have employees, they can set up and contribute to their own IRAs.
- **How to get started:** You can open an IRA at an online brokerage or through a Financial Advisor.
- **Tax advantage:** Tax deduction for contributions if you are not covered by a retirement plan at work.
- **Final thoughts:** An IRA is probably the easiest way for self-employed people to start saving for retirement. There are no special filing requirements, and you can use it whether or not you have employees.

Solo 401k
- **Best for:** A business owner or self-employed person with

no employees (except a spouse, if applicable).

- **Contribution limit:** Up to $57,000 in 2020 (plus $6,500 catch-up contribution for those 50 or older) or 100 percent of earned income, <u>whichever is less</u>. To help understand the contribution limits here, it helps to think of yourself as two people: An employer (of yourself) and an employee (yourself).
  - o In your capacity as the employee, you can contribute as you would to a standard employer-offered 401(k) with salary deferrals of up to 100 percent of your compensation or $19,500 (plus that $6,500 catch-up contribution, if eligible), whichever is less.
  - o In your capacity as the employer, you can make an additional contribution of up to 25 percent of your compensation.
  - o There is a special rule for sole proprietors and those organized as a single-member Limited Liability Company (LLC): You can contribute 25 percent of net self-employment income, which is your net profit less half your self-employment tax and the plan contributions you made for yourself.
  - o The limit on compensation that can be used to factor your contribution is $285,000 in 2020.
- **Employee element:** You cannot contribute to a solo 401(k) if you have employees. But you can hire your spouse so he or she can also contribute to the plan. Your spouse can contribute up to the standard employee 401(k) contribution limit, plus you can add in the employer contributions, for up to an additional $57,000 total, plus catch-up contribution, if eligible. Saving as a couple potentially doubles what you can save.
- **How to get started:** You can open a solo 401(k) at many online brokers and via a Financial Advisor. You will need to file paperwork with the IRS each year once you have more than $250,000 in your account.
- **Tax advantage:** This plan works just like a standard, employer-offered 401(k): You make contributions pre-

tax, and distributions after age 59½ are taxed as ordinary income (i.e. similar to wage/W2 income).

- **Final thoughts:** This plan, which the IRS calls a "one-participant 401(k)," is particularly attractive for those who can and want to save a great deal of money for retirement or those who want to save a lot in some years - say, when business is flush - and less in others. Keep in mind that the contribution limits apply per person, not per plan. So, if you also have outside employment that offers a 401(k), or your spouse does, the contribution limits apply to both plans.

Simplified Employee Pension (SEP)

- **Best for:** Self-employed people or small-business owners with no or few employees.
- **Contribution limit:** The lesser of $57,000 in 2020 or up to 25 percent of compensation or net self-employment earnings with a $285,000 limit on compensation that can be used to factor the contribution. Again, net self-employment income is net profit less half of your self-employment taxes paid and your SEP contribution. No catch-up contribution is allowed.
- **Employee element:** Employers must contribute an equal percentage of salary for each eligible employee, and you are counted as an employee. That means if you contribute 15 percent of your compensation for yourself, you must contribute 15 percent of each eligible employee's compensation.
- **How to get started:** You can open a SEP IRA at many online brokers or via a Financial Advisor just as you would a traditional or Roth IRA. There are a few extra pieces of paperwork, but they are not complex.
- **Tax advantage:** You can deduct the lesser of your contributions or 25 percent of net self-employment earnings or compensation - limited to that $285,000 cap per employee in 2020 - on your tax return. Distributions

in retirement are taxed as ordinary income.

- **Final thoughts:** A SEP IRA is easier than a solo 401(k) to maintain - there is a low administrative burden with limited paperwork and no annual reporting to the IRS - and has similarly high contribution limits. Like the solo 401(k), SEP IRAs are flexible in that you do not have to contribute every year. The downside for you, as the business owner, is that you have to make contributions for employees, and they must be equal to the ones you make for yourself. That can be costly if you have more than a few employees or if you would like to put away a great deal for your own retirement. You cannot simply use a SEP to save for yourself; if you contribute for the year, you have to make contributions for all eligible employees.

SIMPLE IRA

- **Best for:** Larger businesses with up to 100 employees.
- **Contribution limit:** Up to $13,500 in 2020 plus catch-up contributions of up to $3,000 if 50 or older. If you also contribute to an employer plan, the total of all contributions cannot exceed $19,500.
- **Employee element:** Unlike the SEP IRA, the contribution burden is not solely on you: employees can contribute through salary deferral. But employers are generally required to make either matching contributions to employee accounts of up to 3 percent of employee compensation or fixed contributions of 2 percent to every eligible employee. Choosing the latter means the employee does not have to contribute to earn your contribution. The compensation limit for factoring contributions is $285,000 in 2020.
- **How to get started:** The process is similar to a SEP IRA - you can open a SIMPLE at an online broker or via a Financial Advisor, with a heavier paperwork load than your standard IRA.
- **Tax advantage:** Contributions are deductible, but

distributions in retirement are taxed as ordinary income. Contributions made to employee accounts are deductible as a business expense.

* **Final thoughts:** If you are the owner of a midsize company with fewer than 100 employees, the SIMPLE IRA is a fairly good option as it is easy to set up, and the accounts are owned by the employees. SIMPLE IRA contribution limits are significantly lower than a SEP IRA or solo 401(k), however, and you may end up having to make mandatory contributions to employee accounts, which can be expensive if you have a large number of employees who participate.

Section 179 expensing

When you buy property, like a vehicle or machinery, for use in your business, you can receive a tax deduction for doing so. These deductions take the form of what is called depreciation. Depreciation basically takes the expense of buying property and spreads it out over a certain number of years. The good thing is that these deductions can save you money on your business tax return.

But an even better deduction is when you take the entire expense in the year when you first buy and begin using this property. This is referred to as a "Section 179 deduction" because of the reference to the corresponding section of the Internal Revenue Code. You can see that there is a benefit to taking the full deduction for the cost of the item immediately, rather than being required to spread out the deduction over the item's useful life. For example, if you buy a computer or other office equipment for your office, under Section 179 you can deduct the full cost of that computer in one year. This also makes practical sense, because we all know that computers have a short lifetime or useful life.

So, what types of business property does Section 179 apply to? The IRS has two general requirements:

1. The property must be "tangible, depreciable, personal property which is acquired for use in the active conduct of a trade or business." Vehicles and (starting in 2018) certain <u>nonresidential</u> real property improvements are also included.

2. The property must be purchased and put into service in the year in which you claim the deduction. Putting an asset into service means that you have it set up and working and you are using it in your business before December 31st. Buying a piece of property and then letting it sit and gather dust does not count.

What does this look like in practice? Well, the following items are some of the most commonly expensed under a Section 179 deduction:

- Equipment (machines, etc.) purchased for business use
- Business Vehicles with a gross vehicle weight in excess of 6,000 lbs.
- Computers
- "Off-the-Shelf" Computer Software
- Office Furniture
- Office Equipment
- Property attached to your building that is not a structural component of the building (i.e. a printing press, large manufacturing tools, and equipment)
- Listed property that can be used for both business and personal purposes. (The 179 deduction is based only on the percentage of time you use this property for business purposes.)
- Costs of improvements to business buildings for fire suppression, alarms, security systems, HVAC, and roofing

For property that qualifies, simply complete Part I of IRS

Form 4562, *Depreciation and Amortization*, when preparing your tax return. However, keep this in mind:

- The maximum Section 179 deduction cannot exceed the taxpayer's business income. If this limit prevents an individual taxpayer from deducting all or part of the cost of Section 179 property, the disallowed amount is carried over to the next tax year.
- The total Section 179 deduction in 2020 (for 2019 tax returns) is $1,020,000. Also, the maximum Section 179 expense deduction for sport utility vehicles placed in service in tax years beginning in 2019 is $25,500.

Turn your car into a tax-deductible goldmine

When it comes to the use of a vehicle in your business, you can figure your deduction using one of two methods. You can either take the amount of your actual expenses or multiply the standard mileage rate by the number of miles driven for business. The IRS will allow you to use either method, so it is wise to calculate your deduction using both methods and use the one that reduces your tax liability the most. However, to use the standard mileage rate, it must be used in the first year the auto is available for use in the taxpayer's business. In subsequent years, the taxpayer can choose to use either the standard mileage rate or actual expenses.

Now that we have that out of the way, what does the standard mileage rate include? It is a substitute for tracking deprecation, lease payments, maintenance, repairs, gasoline, oil changes, insurance, and vehicle registration fees.[5] Please note that above the standard mileage rate, you can separately deduct vehicle interest expense on an auto loan, parking fees and tolls, as well as personal property taxes based on the value of the car.[6] Due to what the rate includes and its ease of tracking/calculation, most people simply choose to take the mileage deduction. They do so by taking the business miles driven and multiplying them by the mileage rate in effect for that year (e.g. $0.575 per mile in 2020).

Example: Aaronita is a broker whose business is organized as a sole proprietorship. She drives her car 23,849 miles during 2020, of which 17,849 were for business. She can take a standard mileage deduction of $10,263 on Schedule C of Form 1040 or she can apply her business percentage of 74.8 percent (17,849/23,849) to her actual expenses and deduct that amount.

Vehicle depreciation

The goal of this book is not to make you an accountant. As such, I am not going to go too deep with regards to depreciation. However, there are some important things that you should know about it so when you are making decisions, you will be well informed.

- Depreciation is nothing more than a pro-rata deduction of an asset's cost over a specified useful life.
- There are two basic depreciation methods:
  - o "Straight-line," which is slower and allows you to deduct in equal amounts
  - o "Accelerated," which allows for faster deductions in the early years.
- If the vehicle is used 50 percent or less for business, the straight-line method must be used.
- For vehicles placed in service in 2019 that cost more than $50,500, the first-year depreciation is limited or capped.
- If the taxpayer does not claim bonus depreciation, the greatest allowable depreciation deduction is:
  - o $10,100 for the first year,
  - o $16,100 for the second year,
  - o $9,700 for the third year, and
  - o $5,760 for each later taxable year in the recovery period.
- If a taxpayer claims 100 percent bonus depreciation, the

greatest allowable depreciation deduction is:
o $18,100 for the first year,
o $16,100 for the second year,
o $9,700 for the third year, and
o $5,760 for each later taxable year in the recovery period.

In Chapter 3, I will talk about how you can bulletproof your mileage deduction via a logbook. Because, if you do not document how you arrived at your vehicle expense deduction, you can rest assured that the IRS will disallow it if you are ever audited!

Leveraging the home office deduction
In today's fast paced, ever connected, and always on, environment, it is not uncommon for most brokers to do work at home. The nature of some deals is that they come quick, and responses are needed immediately to move forward. So, even if you have an office available to you and you pay desk fees, you still may have to work from home occasionally. For home office expenses, self-employed individuals can expense a portion of keeping up their home as well as the related workspace expenditures. Unfortunately, home office expenses are audited frequently by the IRS because they have figured out, through much experience, that this is where some taxpayers tend to cheat. So, in this section, I will discuss the basics of the deduction and tell you how to protect it from IRS scrutiny later in Chapter 3.

So, the first thing to know is that if you have a home office, the IRS states that the workspace must be used *regularly* and *exclusively* for business. This means that the workspace cannot be used for anything else; it must be used 100 percent for business. According to the IRS, this means that to qualify to deduct expenses for business use of your home, you must use that part of your home:[7]

- Exclusively and regularly as a place where you meet or deal with patients, clients, or customers in the normal course of your trade or business;
- In the case of a separate structure which is not attached to your home, in connection with your trade or business;
- On a regular basis for certain storage use;
- For rental use; or
- As a daycare facility.

The IRS has routinely disallowed expenses claimed for desks in kitchens and dining rooms, dens, playrooms, entire basements, and the like. Once the above hurdle is cleared, the next thing to do is to determine what expenses to deduct.

The home office deduction basically works like this: take the square footage of your office, divide it by the square footage of the house, and apply that percentage to all of the expenses associated with the home and your business. Any expenses directly related to the office are deducted at a rate of 100 percent. A simplified version would look like **Figure 2-1**. To claim the deduction of $3,001 shown, you would then complete IRS Form 8829, *Expenses for Business Use of Your Home*. The expense would then flow to Schedule C where it would reduce your profit and associated tax liability.

What if you do not feel like going through the hassle of tallying up all your housing related expenses? The IRS will allow you to use what it calls the "simplified method"[8] to calculate your deduction. Simply take the square footage of your office (limited to 300 square feet), multiply it by $5 and "voila!" you have your deduction. In our example, the taxpayer would get a deduction of $900 (i.e. 180 x $5). But as you can see, it is $2,101 LESS than if they take the time to calculate it via Form 8829. So, simplicity does have its tradeoffs.

House Expenses	Direct Expenses	Indirect Expenses
Home office square footage	180	
Total area of home	2,489	
Business use percentage	7.23%	

House Expenses	Direct Expenses	Indirect Expenses
Mortgage interest or rent		$16,489
Real estate taxes		$3,800
Insurance		$841
Repairs and maintenance	$212	
Utilities:		
Electric		$690
Gas		$1,400
Water		$228
Internet and cable		$1,848
Business phone line	$960	
Total	$1,172	$25,296
Business use percentage		7.23%
Total direct and indirect expenses	$1,172	$1,829
Allowable business use of home deduction		$3,001

Figure 2-1

Author's note: Inevitably the question always comes up when speaking to brokers, "Can I still take the home office deduction if I have a desk that I regularly use at the brokerage?" In these instances, the answer will depend on where the broker does their administrative work. The IRS and tax courts have ruled that your home office can qualify as your principal place for deducting expenses if:

- You use it exclusively and regularly for administrative[9] or management activities of your trade or business.
- You have no other fixed location where you conduct substantial administrative or management activities of your trade or business.

Thus, if you perform the following activities at your home

Jared R. Rogers, CPA

office, it is possible to make it your <u>administrative office</u>, which allows you to take the home office deduction for it:

- Billing customers, clients, or patients.
- Keeping books and records.
- Ordering supplies.
- Setting up appointments.
- Forwarding orders or writing reports.

Example: [10] Paul is a self-employed anesthesiologist. He spends the majority of his time administering anesthesia and postoperative care in three local hospitals. One of the hospitals provides him with a small shared office where he could conduct administrative or management activities.

Paul very rarely uses the office the hospital provides. He uses a room in his home that he has converted to an office. He uses this room exclusively and regularly to conduct all the following activities.

- Contacting patients, surgeons, and hospitals regarding scheduling.
- Preparing for treatments and presentations.
- Maintaining billing records and patient logs.
- Satisfying continuing medical education requirements.
- Reading medical journals and books.

Paul's home office qualifies as his principal place of business for deducting expenses for its use. He conducts administrative or management activities for his business as an anesthesiologist there, and he has no other fixed location where he conducts substantial administrative or management activities for this business. His choice to use his home office instead of the one provided by the hospital does not disqualify his home office from being his principal place of business. His performance of substantial non-administrative or non-management activities at fixed locations outside his home also does not disqualify his home office from being his principal place of business. He meets all the qualifications, including principal place of business, so he can deduct expenses (subject to certain limitations, explained later) for the business use of his home.

Health insurance for the self-employed

Do you pay for health insurance? Health insurance paid on behalf of a self-employed taxpayer is deductible as an adjustment to income on line 16 of IRS Schedule 1 (Form 1040), *Additional Income and Adjustments to Income*. Deductible amounts include health insurance premiums paid for the self-employed taxpayer, spouse, dependents, and a child under age 27, if any of the following apply:

- The taxpayer was self-employed and had a net profit for the year (including self-employment earnings from a partnership).
- The taxpayer used one of the optional methods to figure net earnings from self-employment on Schedule SE.

If you paid insurance premiums, consider taking them as an adjustment on Form 1040 versus using them as an itemized deduction on Schedule A. You may benefit more from this treatment, especially if your Adjusted Gross Income (AGI) places you at a level where expenses would not be deductible on Schedule A due to them not exceeding the medical expense floor.

Author's note: All Medicare Parts (e.g. Parts A, B, C, & D) are insurance constituting medical care eligible for the self-employed health insurance deduction.[11] If you find that you did not use them to claim the deduction in prior years, know that you can amend open years to claim the deduction.

What about brokers who organize their businesses as S-Corps? Are they allowed a health insurance deduction? The short answer is yes, but the taxpayer must receive wages from a S-Corp in which they are more than a 2 percent shareholder. To get the deduction:

- The S-Corp must pay for the insurance premiums, either directly or through reimbursement.
- The premiums paid for the health insurance must be shown as wages in box 1 of the employee's W2.
- You then deduct the expense on Schedule 1 as outlined above.

Health insurance is an expensive item. For some, even if it is claimed on Schedule A, it may not yield any tax benefit. If you are self-employed, taking it as an adjustment on the face of Form 1040, might lower your income tax bill!

The 20 Percent Qualified Business Income Deduction

The TCJA created a new 20 percent deduction for pass-through businesses. This deduction is also known as the Section 199A deduction and the deduction for qualified business income (QBI). To be eligible, you must have QBI from a "qualified" trade or business, which most brokers typically would be considered as having. From an "entity" standpoint, the following are those that may be able to take the deduction:

- Sole proprietorships (i.e. Schedule C filers)
- LLCs
- S-Corporations
- Partnerships
- Real estate investors
- Trusts, estates, REITs, and qualified cooperatives

If you file a Schedule C or receive a Schedule K-1 from one of the above entities, then you will report the income and claim the 20 percent deduction on your Form 1040. There can be some complications surrounding the deduction calculations, but most do not apply if your 2019 income was below $160,700 for single filers or $321,400 for those who are married filing jointly. So, what does all of this mean? Effectively, you can earn $100,000 in 2019 and pay the same amount of tax as you would have if you only earned $80,000 before the TCJA was implemented! Since this is automatically a part of the tax law, other than making sure the deduction shows up on line 10 of your Form 1040, there is nothing else to do. However, if you make over the thresholds specified above, it would be best to consult a tax professional to ensure the deduction is calculated accurately.

SUMMARY

- Do not leave money on the table. Make sure you review, track, and take all of the deductions you are legally allowed.

- One can generally deduct 50 percent of the cost of meals associated with dining with potential customers, clients, or other business contacts.

- Meals provided to employees or as part of advertising presentations to the general public are typically 100 percent deductible.

- The cost of entertaining clients and business associates is no longer deductible under the TCJA.

- Brokers have many options when it comes to contributing to retirement accounts. Yet, most of them afford you a tax deduction, so they should strongly be considered within one's tax planning strategy.

- If you purchase machinery, equipment, or office furniture that is used in connection with your business, consider expensing it the year you put it in service via a Section 179 deduction.

- Brokers may be able to take a home office deduction, even if they have a desk or space that they use at their brokerage.

- Do the calculations to take the deduction the "long" way via Form 8829 as well as via the "simplified" method and use the one that yields the biggest tax savings.

- Health insurance is an expensive item. If you pay for insurance in connection with your business, taking it as an adjustment on the face of Form 1040 might lower your income tax bill.

- Make sure that you are getting the 20 Percent Qualified Business Income Deduction before you file your tax return. If you make over the thresholds outlined, consult a tax professional to ensure the deduction is calculated accurately.

NOTES

[1] Department of the Treasury, Internal Revenue Service, Notice 2018-76, (Washington, DC: 2018), https://www.irs.gov/pub/irs-drop/n-18-76.pdf

[2] 26 U.S. Code § 162. Trade or business expenses. Available online at https://www.law.cornell.edu/uscode/text/26/162. (Accessed January 11, 2020).

[3] 26 U.S. Code § 274(e). Disallowance of certain entertainment, etc., expenses. Available online at https://www.law.cornell.edu/uscode/text/26/274. (Accessed January 11, 2020).

[4] Social Security Administration. "Benefits Paid By Type Of Beneficiary." SSA.gov. https://www.ssa.gov/OACT/ProgData/icp.html (Accessed December 4, 2019).

[5] Department of the Treasury, Internal Revenue Services, Publication 463, *Travel, Gift, and Car Expenses* (Washington, DC: 2019), https://www.irs.gov/pub/irs-pdf/p463.pdf.

[6] Ibid.

[7] 26 U.S. Code § 280(A)(c). Exceptions for certain business or rental use; limitation on deductions for such use. Available online at https://www.law.cornell.edu/uscode/text/26/280A. (Accessed January 11, 2020).

[8] Department of the Treasury, Internal Revenue Service, Publication 587, *Business Use of Your Home,* (Washington, DC: 2019), https://www.irs.gov/pub/irs-pdf/p587.pdf.

[9] Ibid.

[10] Ibid.

[11] Department of the Treasury, Internal Revenue Service, Office of Chief Counsel, Memorandum 201228037. *Deductibility of Medicare Premiums Under Code Section 162(l),* (Washington, DC: 2012), https://www.irs.gov/pub/irs-wd/1228037.pdf

CHAPTER 3
How to Audit Proof Your Deductions

The last thing you want to do is stick red flags all over your tax return inviting the IRS to take a closer look. To that end, is there actually a way to "audit-proof" a tax return? Is there a strategy for preparing your return to guarantee that you will not be subject to an audit? Of course not! But there certainly are ways to minimize your risk. In this chapter, I discuss some overarching steps (as well as some detailed actions) you can take to protect the deductions most commonly taken by brokers (and routinely audited by the IRS).

To lessen the likelihood that your return is selected for review (i.e. examination), keep the following in mind before you submit it:

- **Consider filing electronically** – When you file electronically, the initial review (if any) will be performed by a computer, not a human. Less human intervention could lower your audit risk.
- **Be neat** – If you do file via paper, be neat. Either use a computer program to complete the forms, or do a review to make sure everything is legible. A messy return (cross-outs, sloppy handwriting, etc.) is like hanging a sign on your return that says, "Audit me!" It might also give the IRS the impression that you are careless and disorganized.
- **Check ID numbers** – Make sure that you have the correct Social Security numbers for everyone on your return.
- **Report amounts for all tax documents received** – Make sure that the figures reported for wages, interest, dividends, pensions, and annuities match those received on your Form W-2 and 1099. Reason? IRS computers match returns against these forms and will flag any discrepancies for adjustment and potential examination.

- *Watch Schedule C losses* - Avoid filing an income tax return with a Schedule C that reports a net loss. This is especially true if your main source of income comes from W-2 wages. In order for these business losses to stand up, you must pass both the "passive loss" and "hobby loss" rules. Not familiar with those rules? Neither are most taxpayers, and the IRS knows it.
- *Avoid excessive or questionable deductions* – The IRS will be suspicious if you claim a large amount of deductions relative to your income or if the deductions are not typical for your type or size of business. Excessive meal, travel, and entertainment expenses and vehicle mileage often set off alarms.
- *Do not use round numbers* - For example, if you report $1,000 or $12,000 instead of $988 or $12,187, it is an indication that you are estimating rather than keeping good records and reporting the actual, correct amount.
- *Check your calculations* – Technology is a beautiful thing, but it is no substitute for human review. Always review your return when complete to ensure that wage totals appear accurate, withholding amounts are computed correctly, and everything appears as it should.

The importance of record keeping

The quickest way to pay too much in taxes is to keep poor records. Without adequate records, you can forget how much you paid for certain items. Humans tend to underestimate things, so you would be putting yourself at a disadvantage by simply trying to "remember" it all. Combine that with the fact that the IRS may audit your return, and you really place yourself at risk of paying more taxes than you should!

If the IRS examines any of your tax returns, you may be asked to explain the items reported. A complete set of records will speed up the examination and lessen the likelihood of the IRS disallowing any of your expenses or deductions. You may ask, "Wait, the IRS can disallow an expense if I do not have support?" Yup! Maintaining adequate records is a matter of tax law[1] that states:

"Every person liable for any tax imposed by this title, or for the collection thereof, shall keep such records, render such statements, make such returns, and comply with such rules and regulations as the Secretary may from time to time prescribe. Whenever in the judgment of the Secretary it is necessary, he may require any person, by notice served upon such person or by regulations, to make such returns, render such statements, or keep such records, as the Secretary deems sufficient to show whether or not such person is liable for tax under this title."

What all the above means (in plain English) is that if you cannot support an item that was claimed on your tax return, the IRS will assume it was made up and remove it. This action will effectively increase your taxable income for the year in question and usually results in the IRS sending you a bill for tax owed.

With that being said, keep the following points in mind when it comes to your business records:

- Generally speaking, you should keep any information that you and the IRS need to determine your correct tax. To that end, if there is a number shown on your Schedule C, you should have support to prove how it was derived or calculated.
- If you are not incorporated, consider getting a separate bank account for your broker related activities. This will easily help you keep your income and expenses segregated from those that are personal. Likewise, it will make it easy for you or your accountant to pull together an income and expense summary at tax time.
- To prove items paid with cash, you should keep some documentation that proves the amount, who the expense was paid to (i.e. the person's or company's name), and the

transaction date.

- To substantiate expenses paid with check, keep either a copy of the canceled check or a statement (or record such as a carbon copy of the check) that shows the check number, amount, payee's name, and the date the check amount was posted to your account by the financial institution.

- For those items paid via a credit card, you need to have records that show the amount charged, the payee's name, and the date of the transaction.

- Account statements from your financial institution are acceptable as proof if they provide the information shown above. If they do not, the IRS can (and will) sometimes disallow the expense.

- When it comes to how long to keep your records, just know that it generally will be until the statute of limitations expires. These statutes are generally 3 years from the date you filed the tax return. However, this is extended to 6 years if you do not report income that you should have, and the omitted income is more than 25 percent of the gross income on the return.

- If you are found to have filed a fraudulent return, just know that *the statute never runs,* and the IRS has unlimited time to come back and review the data contained within.

- Paper records take up a lot of space, and they can fade or be damaged. As such, many people prefer to keep electronic records. Just remember that all the requirements that apply to hard copy records apply to electronic records, including record retention periods. If you scan or otherwise transfer your tax records to an electronic format, you must be able to store, preserve, retrieve, and reproduce the records in a legible, readable format.

Bulletproof your mileage deduction via a logbook

For many brokers, their cars might feel like their offices as opposed to the one at their brokerage or even at home. Why?

Well, because a broker's car is often an important tool for doing his or her "job." However, I can tell you from experience that the expenses associated with this tool when listed on your tax return (e.g. the mileage deduction) often land people in hot water with the IRS. Like the home office deduction, the IRS knows that 1) many people do not follow the rules for claiming the deduction and, 2) a fair number of people "fudge" their numbers. With that said, this is an area that the IRS audits quite often.

If you are audited, the IRS will ask that you prove your mileage deduction. But do not assume that you can just hand over some scribbles on a sheet of paper, and that will be acceptable. Far from it my friend! You see, the IRS has some pretty strict "substantiation" rules when it comes to this deduction. Essentially, your records must be adequate to support your business use.[2] Per the IRS, an adequate record[3] is one made at or near the time of said business use.[4] *Other sufficient evidence* is acceptable only if you have direct corroborative evidence or other documentary evidence.[5] So, while you do not necessarily need to keep a daily mileage log, it should be completed near or at the time of each event.[6] A weekly log of what you did during the week is also considered acceptable.[7]

If you were to look at Part IV of Schedule C, you will see that there are several questions that the IRS asks taxpayers as it relates to the use of their vehicles. What is important to note is that in order to prove how much you use your vehicle for business, you must be able to provide your:

- Total miles
- Total business miles
- Total commuting miles
- Total other miles (e.g. personal/non-commuting)

Author's note: In order to protect your mileage deduction, it is strongly encouraged that you keep a mileage log. Yes, I know it can be a pain, but the good news is that you have your choice of several types of methods of completing it. The bad news is that I can almost guarantee you that you have not been doing it 100 percent correctly over the years! The methods most commonly used/accepted by the IRS include:

1. The perfect one-day car log
2. The 90-day log
3. The first-week rule

With the perfect one-day log, you would list all your appointments (both business and personal). When you use the car to go to an appointment, you would list the mileage next to it. At the end of the day, you would list your final odometer reading. You would then tally all your business, commuting, and other miles and reconcile them with your beginning and ending odometer readings. The important point is that you would record your business and personal mileage daily for each stop. Out of the three allowable methods, this is the most complicated. An example of this type of mileage log is shown in **Figure 3-1**.

With the 90-day log, what the IRS allows you to do is let a mileage record for a period be representative for an entire year's substantiation.[8] Under this method, you would use a three-month period that is representative of your entire year's mileage activity, and essentially keep the same details reflected in the perfect one day log. The first-week rule operates in a similar manner, except you keep track of your miles during the first week of each month and extrapolate the year that way.

As you can see, no matter how you slice it, the IRS requires that you prove how you arrived at your deduction. If doing any of the above sounds like a lot of work, know that you are correct. But what is it worth to you? Protecting your mileage deduction or letting the IRS disallow it and increase your tax bill? Furthermore, in today's smartphone age, there are many apps that will do all this work for you. While this is most certainly not an endorsement, one of the most widely used is Mile IQ and is worth checking out.

MONTH				
DAY OF THE WEEK S M T W T F S				
DAILY APPOINTMENTS	BUSINESS	COMMUTE	OTHER	
7:00 AM				
7:30 AM				
8:00 AM				
8:30 AM				
9:00 AM				
9:30 AM				
10:00 AM				
10:30 AM				
11:00 AM				
11:30 AM				
12:00 PM				
12:30 PM				
1:00 PM				
1:30 PM				
2:00 PM				
2:30 PM				
3:00 PM				
3:30 PM				
4:00 PM				
4:30 PM				
5:00 PM				
	TOTAL MILES			
	BEG. ODOMETER			
	END ODOMETER			

Figure 3-1

Ensuring your home office deduction is defensible

I am routinely asked by clients and prospects whether the IRS will actually come out to your home to check if you are using a portion of it "exclusively" for business. The answer is yes, and I have heard many stories from various colleagues that it has happened to. One Enrolled Agent (EA) even told me how an IRS Revenue Agent was touring his clients house as part of an audit, and how the EA had to kick the toys of his clients kid under the couch so the agent would not see them and ask why they were in the office! So, what we are going to look at now is how you can protect your deduction. By doing the small things outlined, you will create a paper trail. It will be this body of documentation that will save you should the IRS come knocking and want the proof that backs up your deduction.

Keep Good Records

I think I have beaten the "keep your records" horse to death by now, so this will be brief. For those items that are used to claim the home office deduction (e.g., gas bills, electric bills, phone bills, etc.), keep the support in a file labeled as such. You can keep the items in paper form or electronic form.[9] That way, if you are asked to prove how the amounts on Form 8829, *Expenses for Business Use of Your Home* were derived, you will have the support ready to produce.

Take a Picture

Twice a year, take a photo of your office to establish that it was used for business. It is easy to say that you qualified for the home office deduction. However, it is harder to prove it when the IRS is auditing you for a prior year. How could the agent know what the office looked like back then? How do they know that there were no personal items in it? A photo that has the date (or a way for you to prove it) can easily put that question to rest. There is no need to send the picture to the IRS with your tax return; just keep it in case it is ever needed in the future.

Keep a Work-Activity Log

Showing how much time you spent working in your office is important. Why? Because it establishes that you use it for substantial administrative activities and that you use it routinely. A work activity log can constitute an excellent supporting document in the event of an audit. The log does not need to be elaborate; it just needs to document some important things like date, time of day, amount of time spent working, and the associated activity. Keep this up to date and just file it with your other supporting documents at the end of the year.

Author's note: If you have set your business up as a S-Corp, know that you can still qualify for the home office deduction. However, you have to do a few workarounds to get it. What are they you ask?

- Draft an "accountable plan" agreement for your company. It will outline what expenses are eligible for reimbursement, how they will be paid, etc. A sample plan can be found online, or a tax attorney can create one for you.
- Calculate the percentage of your home that is used exclusively for business purposes. Divide the square footage used for business by the total square footage of the home and multiply by 100.
- Calculate the total amount of eligible reimbursable expenses (see Form 8829). Multiply each amount by the percentage of business use calculated in the step above and enter the results on the expense form that you use for your accountable plan.
- Prepare expense reports as the employee and turn them in to your company on a regular basis. Attach receipts or other documentation to the form to substantiate them.
- Cut the check from the business account and deposit it into your personal account. Attach a copy of the check to the form as documentation that these were paid.
- Enter the amount of the payment into your S-Corp's records as a reimbursement for employee expenses. Post each expense claimed to the appropriate expense account so that these expenses may be deducted from the corporation's income on its tax return.

SUMMARY

- Review the 8 items outlined at the beginning of this chapter before you submit your return each year to reduce your audit risk.

- IRS Publication 583, *Starting a Business and Keeping Records,* is a good guide that lists the types of documentation that the IRS requires you to keep.

- Make sure you keep an IRS compliant mileage logbook to protect your mileage deduction.

- Make sure you take semi-annual pictures of your home office showing that it was used exclusively for business (i.e. no personal items contained in it whatsoever).

- Use a work-activity log to document your time spent in your office routinely doing your administrative activities.

- If you have structured your business as a S-Corp, make sure that you have/use an accountable plan to administer the home office deduction.

NOTES

[1] 26 U.S. Code § 6001. Notice or regulations requiring records, statements, and special returns. Available online at https://www.law.cornell.edu/uscode/text/26/6001. (Accessed January 11, 2020).

[2] 26 U.S. Code § 274-5(d). Disallowance of certain entertainment, etc., expenses. Substantiation required. Available online at https://www.law.cornell.edu/cfr/text/26/1.274-5. (Accessed January 11, 2020).

[3] Ibid.

[4] 26 U.S. Code § 1.274-5T(c)(1) and 1.274-5T(c)(2)(ii)(A).

[5] 26 U.S. Code § 1.274-5T(c)(3)

[6] 26 U.S. Code § 1.274-5T(c)(2)

[7] Ibid.

[8] 26 U.S. Code § 1.274-5T(c)(3)(ii)

[9] Department of the Treasury, Internal Revenue Service, Revenue Procedure 98-25; 1998-1 C.B. 689

CHAPTER 4
Sophisticated Tax Strategies from High Priced Tax Professionals

I have been in this field for many years. Over that course of time, I have learned and seen a lot of things. I have interacted with every level of tax preparer and planner you can imagine. Some are worth their salt and some are not. But those who are tend to have one thing in common. They analyze the taxpayer's situation and look for tax saving opportunities to help them plan for the future – in short, they become that person's partner. In this section, I will discuss some of the best planning strategies I have picked up through the years.

Employing your children

One of the advantages of operating your own business is hiring family members. By doing so, you might be able to reduce your taxes via income shifting, help set them up for retirement, as well as reduce your company's tax bill. But the IRS has some rules that apply to family employees that do not apply to other employee categories. Here, I will make sure you get the biggest tax bang for your buck while not running afoul of the IRS.

The first thing to know is that it is totally within your right as a small business owner for you to employ your children or family members. As a business owner, you can take a deduction for the wages paid to your child, while your child can utilize their standard deduction ($12,400 in tax year 2020) to offset those wages making them income tax-free (and possibly payroll tax-free). So, if you have a child who is of working age and can legitimately perform tasks associated with your business, consider adding them to your payroll roster.

Example: The following example will highlight the various tax savings by implementing some or all of the associated strategies allowed by employing your child.

Let us say a broker is set up as a S-Corp and is in the 35 percent tax bracket. She hires her 15-year-old daughter to work in the office on weekends to help with filing, shredding, cleaning, etc. The child earns $12,400 in wages throughout the year and has no other earnings. Since the full amount of the wages will be deductible as compensation paid by the business, the tax savings to the business owner is $4,340 ($12,400 x 35 percent), and the income tax to the child is $0, since all of these wages are offset by the child's standard deduction.

Even if the wages exceed the standard deduction, the child is allowed to make an IRA contribution up to $6,000 in 2020 which, is an "above the line" deduction and could substantially reduce the child's taxable income. If the maximum traditional IRA contribution is made, the first $18,400 of the child's taxable wages will result in no income tax liability ($12,400 standard deduction + $6,000 IRA deduction). And again, assuming the parent's 35 percent income tax bracket, the child's wages would produce an income tax savings of $6,440 to them.

If wages are paid to the child in excess of the $12,400 standard deduction, any income in excess of the standard deduction will be taxed at the child's tax rate. The lowest tax bracket of 10 percent applies to taxable income up to $9,875 for tax year 2020. Assuming a traditional IRA contribution is not made, the child could earn up to $22,275 ($22,275 - $12,400 standard deduction = $9,875 10 percent bracket limit) before being pushed into the next tax bracket, assuming he or she earns no other income.

Author's note: Here are some things that you will want to consider when employing this strategy:

- If your children are under 18 and you are a sole proprietor or single-member LLC, or run a spousal partnership, your children will not have to pay Social Security or Medicare taxes if they work for you. This can help you avoid paying 15.3 percent of their wages as tax.

- Maintain payroll documentation and records to prove that your children are bona fide employees.
- Be realistic about their skills and compensation as well. The IRS is not likely to believe that a 14-year-old is doing your accounting, and it will keep an eye out for an unreasonably high pay rate.
- If your children are still dependents and their earned income exceeds the standard deduction of $12,400 for 2020, they will have to file their own income tax returns.
- Having earned income will allow your child to contribute to a Roth IRA. Contributions to a Roth IRA are limited to the lesser of the taxpayer's compensation or $6,000. Refer to the discussion in the next topic for more details.

Funding your child's retirement via a Roth account

When it comes to amassing earnings in any investment vehicle (e.g. a 529 plan, IRA, etc.), the most valuable asset one has is time. The longer that the earnings have to compound, the larger the balance will grow. So, what if you could give your child a "tax-free" retirement with an account that had amassed a significant amount? You can if you plan properly.

You see, while it is possible to open a traditional IRA for a minor, there is one sticking point that usually precludes one from opening a Roth IRA instead. The most important thing to know about opening a Roth IRA for a child is that they must have earned money during that tax year. This is because the contribution limit is the lesser of the amount they earned or the IRS prescribed cap.

If a child is of working age and has a job, then they are eligible to open and contribute to a Roth. So, if you are making enough money where you can employ your child and pay them $6,000, then why not? Not only will your business be able to deduct the wages paid, but you can give them a tremendous head start when it comes to retirement. Remember, the wealthy tend to be that way because they pass wealth down to the next generation. Now that you know one of the ways to do so, use it to your advantage.

Author's note: When considering this opportunity, keep the following tips in mind:

- The same rules that decide eligibility for Roth IRAs apply to the account you open for your child. You or another adult will be the custodian on the account, but your child will be the owner.
- It is up to you (or the child) to document that they had income earned from work.
- The contribution made to your child's Roth IRA can be a gift from you or someone else. However, remember to keep the IRS's gift tax rules in mind.
- In a custodial Roth IRA, the adult controlling the account is the only person who can make investment decisions.
- If you begin your kid's Roth IRA with a small amount, like $750, you may need to wait to buy into certain funds due to their "minimum" requirement.
- The benefit of a Roth IRA is that whatever money you earn from your investments will not be taxed when you withdraw it. However, the money must be held in the account for at least five years for this to be achieved.
- Once the child who owns the account turns 18 (or 21 in some states), you can take steps with your brokerage to shift the account into their control.

For more details on when one can contribute to a Roth IRA, AGI limits on contributions as well as other specifics, refer to IRS Publication 590-A, *Contributions to Individual Retirement Arrangements (IRAs)*.

Section 105 Medical Expense Reimbursement Plan

If you are like most "working age" people, you may find that you typically cannot deduct your medical expenses. This is because 1) the deduction only comes into play if you itemize via IRS Schedule A, *Itemized Deductions* and 2) if you do itemize, your expenses have to exceed 7.5 percent of your AGI. For a family with income of $100,000 this would mean that they would have to pay $7,500 in medical expenses before even $1 would be deductible as an itemized deduction. But what if there was a way to potentially deduct all of your medical expenses with no regard to any threshold? Well, you are in luck my friend. Welcome to the Medical Expense Reimbursement Plan (MERP)!

The IRS allows for a MERP to be formed even if the employer only has one employee. Unfortunately, if your business is structured as a sole-proprietorship, then you do not qualify as an employee for the purposes of a MERP.[1] I can hear you saying, "What good does a MERP do me, Jared, as a broker with no employees?" Well, this is why you would consider hiring your spouse or child in your business - so you can deduct medical expenses that would normally not be deductible! Let us now take a look at how a MERP actually works and how you can set it up.

With a MERP, any reimbursements of employee medical expenses that your business pays are 100 percent tax deductible to the employer (you). What is even better is that they reduce your tax liability. The employer has full control of the design of this plan and can make it as narrow or broad as they like. For example, you can cover such expenses as deductibles, copays, orthodontics, dental, mileage to and from the doctor, routine physicals, psychiatric treatment, and nontraditional medicine such as acupuncture, chiropractic, etc. that are not covered by insurance. So, if your spouse is your only employee, then your company would reimburse them for all these out of pocket expenses. Furthermore, if they elect "family coverage" when they sign up, they can get reimbursed for expenses incurred by any member of their family (i.e. you).

If this sounds interesting to you, here are the steps to set up a MERP:

- If you are married and your business is a sole proprietorship or LLC, hire your spouse. If you are not married, form a regular corporation and have the corporation approve the plan in the board of director's minutes.
- Have the MERP drafted and reviewed by an attorney. Both you and the employee should sign and date it to memorialize when it became effective and implemented.
- If you have hired your spouse, make them the primary insured on the plan and elect family coverage; which means that you will be covering yourself and any kids as well.
- Either pay the doctor or dentist directly or reimburse the family member for any medical expenses incurred. The bottom line is that you get a deduction and your family gets the money tax-free!
- Keep the plan in existence for at least 3 years.
- Make sure that you keep records of employee hours worked in case the IRS comes knocking and wants proof that work was done. A simple time sheet noting the days, hours, and nature of work performed should suffice.

Author's note: As you are probably quickly getting used to by now, there are always some details that you should be aware of. So, with a MERP, make sure you consider:

- S-Corps get most of the benefits provided to sole-proprietorships. However, if you are more than a 2 percent owner of a S-Corp or a partner in a partnership, you do not get the benefits of the MERP.

- A MERP cannot discriminate in favor of the owners or highly compensated employees. With that said, if your MERP covers all employees, then that effectively eliminates any problems.
- If you are reimbursing an employee, make sure they submit the expenses to the business (i.e. you) and that you keep the records as proof of what was paid. This will help you if the IRS asks.
- This is not something that you wait until April 14th to try and run up the flagpole in an effort to reduce your tax bill. Make sure that you set this in motion well before the tax year ends and that you have maintained the documentation as previously outlined.

Understanding the S-Corp election and late filing relief

What is presented in this section could possibly be the second most impactful tax strategy you learn. It is often one that I charge clients a significant amount of money to employ. However, you are going to get it for the price of admission via your book purchase! What am I referring to? Making the IRS election to be taxed as a S-Corporation (S-Corp).

Unless you converted from a regular corporation to a S-Corp,[2] then a S-Corp is not subject to Federal income tax.[3] The way that this entity works is very similar to if you were set up as a sole-proprietor. The S-Corp tallies up its gross income and subtracts its business deductions to arrive at the net taxable income. However, depending on how many owners there are, those individuals then claim and report their pro-rata share of the S-Corp's income or loss on their individual return.

Example: Pilar is a 50 percent shareholder in a S-Corp. The corporation had gross sales of $575,000 and deductions of $425,000, for a net income of $150,000. Since Pilar owns 50 percent of the stock, she would report 50 percent of the profit on her tax return (i.e. $75,000) and be responsible for paying the income tax associated with it.

Unfortunately, Pilar must pay the income tax on her share of the company's net income whether the cash was distributed to her or not. Thus, if her $75,000 was left in the company to fund future growth, Pilar would still have to pay income tax on it. So, you may be wondering what is so great about a S-Corp from a tax perspective? Let us get to the meat of it, shall we?

With a S-Corp, you pay Social Security and Medicare taxes on the wages, salaries, and bonuses that the company pays to its employees. This includes wages that are paid to employee owners. However, distributions and undistributed earnings are not subject to these taxes. Moreover, this is where the important difference lies. If a broker organizes his or her activity as a sole proprietorship and reports the net income via Schedule C, not only will he or she pay income tax on the profit but **also** self-employment tax.

Self-employment tax, which is paid at a rate of 15.3 percent, represents both the employee and employer contributions for Social Security (6.2 percent) and Medicare (1.45 percent) taxes. When you work as a W-2 employee, you have 7.65 percent withheld from your check and your employer matches the other 7.65 percent. Yet, when you organize your activity as a S-Corp, the net income of the company is only subject to the income tax.

Example: Let us assume the same fact pattern as the example for Pilar, except she is the only owner and she is structured as a sole proprietor. She generated $150,000 in revenue and had $75,000 in expenses. This leaves her with $75,000 of profit, just as it did above. But due to her structure, she will pay income tax on the $75,000 **as well as** 15.3 percent self-employment tax, or approximately $10,597.[4] Ouch!

If you are still following the examples, then a very logical question comes up. Why not just structure your activity as a S-Corp, pay zero salary, and take all the earnings as distributions and completely eliminate all self-employment tax? Unfortunately, the IRS has thought of this.[5] The IRS requires shareholder employees to pay themselves "reasonable" compensation. If you do not, the entire amount of distributions can be reclassified as wages, which are fully subject to self-employment tax. In fact, just about all taxpayers who did not understand this rule have ended up losing when they challenged it in tax court!

With that being said, astute tax professionals will typically advise you to pay yourself as little salary as possible and take the remainder as a distribution.

Example: Samantha has net income of $60,000 from her S-Corp. If all of this was paid to her in the form of salary, it would be subject to self-employment tax at the rate of 15.3 percent or $9,180. If, however, Sam pays herself a salary of $30,000 and takes the other $30,000 as a distribution then the savings on the self-employment tax be $4,590! Not bad, huh?

So, the next logical question is what does the IRS consider "reasonable compensation" for its purposes? Well, the IRS defines it as what one would ordinarily be paid for like services, by like enterprises, under like circumstances.[6] This is generally understood to mean "what would you pay an outside agency or person to do the same duties?" However, there are several factors that determine what is reasonable such as:

- Responsibilities involved
- Time spent performing above responsibilities
- Actual services performed
- Size and complexity of the business
- Salary paid to company officers in prior years
- Prevailing economic conditions

You may still be wondering, "Jared, can you just give me a flat number or percentage of income that I will be "okay" paying myself to have it considered reasonable?" Unfortunately, I cannot. But I can give you two things to consider. Based on several court cases I have researched, many of the rulings considered a salary that was paid as reasonable when it was between approximately 40 percent and 60 percent of net income.[7] Second, there are plenty of companies out there that you can pay for a "reasonable compensation study" to determine what could be used for your company.

Author's note: A S-Corp is formed in the same manner as any other business corporation. A corporation may be formed under state law, or an eligible non-corporate entity may elect to be taxed as a corporation. Yet what is important is that the S-Corp election **is made with the IRS, not the state**. The election to be taxed as a corporation is made by filing IRS Form 2553, *Election by a Small Business Corporation*. This form is time bound. For your election to be effective:

- The date you incorporated – file the form no later than two months and 15 days after the incorporation date.
- The following year – any time during the preceding year, but no later than two months and 15 days (e.g. March 15th) of the year it is to be effective.

If you miss the deadline to file Form 2553, all hope is not lost. You may be able to still be granted S-Corp status up to three years and 75 days after you wanted the election to be effective. IRS "Revenue Procedure 2013-30" provides guidance for relief for late S-Corp elections. I would recommend you employ a good accountant or tax attorney if you find yourself in this situation.

The IRS real estate professional designation
It is common for many brokers to also own real estate. As

many real estate investors quickly discover, rental real estate has the amazing power to potentially provide tax losses/deductions with tax free cash flow on top of a building. However, rental activities are automatically classified as passive activities by the IRS regardless of the taxpayer's level of participation. What this means is that losses from a "passive activity" may only be used to offset income from another passive activity. Any remaining losses in excess of passive income for a particular tax year are often disallowed and carried forward to future years. Yet, if a taxpayer or spouse actively participates in a passive rental real estate activity, a loss deduction of up to $25,000 may be allowed if certain requirements are met.

An important detail about the $25,000 loss deduction is that it is impacted by a person's AGI. The deduction starts to get phased out when your AGI is above $100,000 and completely vanishes once it exceeds $150,000. I will discuss this more in Chapter 6 when I talk about tax deductions available to landlords. But what if you are considered a real estate professional? Well, then the $25,000 loss limitation, $100,000 AGI test, and the $100,000 through $150,000 phase out rules do not apply. This means that you are able to deduct 100 percent of your rental depreciation and "losses" against ANY other type of income on the front page of your 1040. So, as you can see, everyone would prefer to qualify as real estate professional.

But what does it take to qualify as such? The following points are key:

1. Were more than half the personal services the taxpayer performed in all trades or businesses during the tax year performed in real property trades or businesses in which the taxpayer materially participated, and
2. Did the taxpayer perform more than 750 hours of services during the tax year in real property trades or businesses in

which the taxpayer materially participated?

A taxpayer who passes both tests is considered a qualifying real estate professional. Now, one of the biggest questions I am often asked is what occupations qualify as real property trades or businesses? Those most commonly noted are real property development, redevelopment, construction, reconstruction, acquisition, conversion, rental, operation, management, leasing, or brokerage. The next question I usually hear is what constitutes material participation? Per the IRS this means:

1. The individual participates in the activity for more than 500 hours during the tax year;
2. The individual's participation in the activity for the tax year constitutes substantially all of the participation in such activity of all individuals (including individuals who are not owners of interests in the activity) for the year;
3. The individual participates in the activity for more than 100 hours during the tax year, and the individual's participation in the activity for the tax year is not less than the participation in the activity of any other individuals (including individuals who are not owners of interests in the activity) for the year;
4. The activity is a significant participation activity for the tax year, and the individual's aggregate participation in all significant participation activities during the year exceeds 500 hours;
5. The individual materially participated in the activity for any five tax years (whether or not consecutive) during the 10 tax years that immediately precede the tax year;
6. The activity is a personal service activity, and the individual materially participated in the activity for any three tax years (whether or not consecutive) preceding the tax year; or
7. Based on all of the facts and circumstances, the individual participates in the activity on a regular, continuous, and substantial basis during the year.

In conclusion, if you work in a real trade and business, materially participate in your activity and perform more than 750 hours of services during the tax year in your real property trades or businesses, you will be able to deduct far more in rental property losses than most taxpayers (which will help cut your tax bill).

SUMMARY

- If you have a child of working age, putting them on your company's payroll can be a good tax strategy.
- You can pay your child up to the standard deduction ($12,400 in tax year 2020) before they will have to pay any Federal income tax.
- Providing your child wage income via Form W2 can allow them to contribute to either a traditional or Roth IRA.
- If you hire your spouse, you can establish a MERP for your business. This will allow you to deduct medical expenses that normally may not be deductible[1]
- By structuring your business as a S-Corp, you can potentially reduce your tax liabilities by eliminating self-employment taxes.
- If you fail to timely make your S-Corp election, you may be able to still be granted S-Corp status up to three years and 75 days after you wanted the election to be effective.
- Being classified as a real estate professional allows you to deduct 100 percent of your depreciation and "losses" from your rental property activities against ANY other type of income on the front page of your 1040.

NOTES

[1] 26 U.S. Code § 105(g). Amounts received under accident and health plans; Self-employed individual not considered an employee. Available online at https://www.law.cornell.edu/uscode/text/26/105. (Accessed January 11, 2020).

[2] 26 U.S. Code § 1374(a). Tax imposed on certain built-in gains. Available online at https://www.law.cornell.edu/uscode/text/26/1374. (Accessed January 11, 2020). Note: This deals with built-in gains where you have accumulated earnings and

profits for a regular corporation. If you started as an S-Corp or never operated your entity as a regular corporation, this is not an issue for you.

[3] 26 U.S. Code § 1363(a). Effect of election on corporation. Available online at https://www.law.cornell.edu/uscode/text/26/1363. (Accessed January 11, 2020).

[4] Due to the way that IRS Form Schedule SE attempts to give credit to a self-employed person for the deduction of employment taxes that an employer would take on wages paid, the 15.3 percent is not charged or calculated on 100 percent of net income. Thus, the actual tax in this example (as reflected on the tax return) would be $75,000 x 92.35 percent x 15.3 percent or $10,597.

[5] Revenue Ruling 74-44, 1974-1 CB 287.

[6] 26 U.S. Code § 1.162-7(b)(3). Compensation for personal services. Available online at https://www.law.cornell.edu/cfr/text/26/1.162-7. (Accessed January 11, 2020).

[7] *Hamilton & Co., Inv. v. Comm.,* 18 TCM 1959-153. In this case it was stated, "The determination of what constitutes reasonable compensation for personal services actually rendered is not a matter of exact mathematical or other science, but is, rather, a matter of individual judgment."

SECTION II
Things A Broker Should Know About Taxes When Interacting with Clients

CHAPTER 5
The Standard Versus Itemized Deduction

Many taxpayers do not take common deductions – for mortgage interest, charitable donations, or medical expenses. The reason? They do not "itemize" their deductions via Schedule A of Form 1040. However, as a broker, you can be an educator with regard to this when someone is making their home purchase. This is particularly true when the client is a first-time homebuyer. To that end, the point of this chapter will be to give you some ammunition you can use to speak intelligently about some of the tax benefits of purchasing a home when engaging prospects and clients. In turn, this will give you more "selling points" to pass on to them, which should also help you close more deals.

Understanding the difference

When you file your tax return, you usually have a choice whether to take the standard deduction or itemize.[1] The IRS will allow you to use whatever method yields you the biggest benefit for that tax year. Thus, you can take the standard deduction in one year and switch and itemize in another without any penalty or questions. But if you do not do the analysis on which one you should take; you could be leaving money on the table. So for starters, keep these points in mind regarding each methodology:

- The standard deduction is determined based on your filing status.[2]
- If you experience a life event such as the birth of a child, a marriage, a divorce or the loss of a spouse, then your filing status and associated standard deduction could change.
- For tax year 2020, the amount of the standard deduction for each filing status is:
  o $12,400 – Single and Married Filing Separately

- o $24,800 - Married Filing Jointly and Surviving Spouses
- o $18,650 – Head of Household
- You are allowed an "additional deduction" if you are age 65 or older OR blind at the end of the tax year.[3]
- A taxpayer who is age 65 or older and blind would be entitled to a basic standard deduction and an additional standard deduction equal to the sum of the additional amounts <u>for both age and blindness</u>.
- For 2020, the standard deduction amount for an individual who may be claimed as a dependent by another taxpayer (e.g. college student with a part-time job) cannot exceed the greater of $1,100 *or* the sum of $350 and the individual's earned income (not to exceed the regular standard deduction amount).
- If the total allowable amounts spent on the following exceed that of the standard deduction, then a taxpayer will (and should) itemize:
  - o Medical and dental expenses that exceed 7.5 percent of your AGI
  - o State and local income or sales taxes
  - o Real estate taxes
  - o Personal property taxes
  - o Mortgage interest and points
  - o Investment interest
  - o Gifts to charity
  - o Disaster losses from a Federally declared disaster

<u>*Author's note:*</u> Before you finalize your tax return, figure your deductions using both methods. Your math does not have to be exact; you just have to be able to estimate if you have enough deductions to warrant you going through the process of itemizing. Once you have prepared your estimate, choose the methodology that has the higher total as that will allow you to pay the lower amount of tax.

Example: You accepted a new job, moved to a different state and purchased a home in May of 2020. That September, you paid the second installment of property taxes that your county assesses to homeowners. Before you finalize your tax return for that year, you do a quick analysis of whether you should itemize. The standard deduction for your filing status, single, is $12,400. You determine that you paid $3,500 in mortgage interest, $1,250 in property taxes and had $8,600 in state taxes taken out of your paycheck. As these three items total $13,350 versus the $12,400 standard deduction, it would be more advantageous for you to itemize this year.

What a taxpayer can deduct once they can itemize

Above I mentioned what one could deduct if they were to itemize their deductions. Here I will get a little into the weeds as it is the details that often matter when it comes to getting the best tax results via itemizing.

Medical expenses

Most taxpayers know that you can deduct out-of-pocket medical expenses to the extent that they exceed 7.5 percent of their AGI. Those who usually benefit the most from a tax perspective tend to be seniors. But what exactly qualifies as a medical expense? Medical expenses are the costs of diagnosis, cure, mitigation, treatment, or prevention of disease, and the costs for treatments affecting any part or function of the body. They include the costs of equipment, supplies, and diagnostic devices needed for these purposes. Outlined below are some of the obvious (and not so obvious) medical expenses that one may deduct:

- *Abortion*
- *Acupuncture*
- *Alcoholism* - Treatment costs at a therapeutic center for alcohol addiction, including meals and lodging at the center during treatment. Also includes transportation to and from AA meetings, if attending meetings on medical advice.

- *Ambulance*
- *Artificial Limb*
- *Artificial Teeth*
- *Bandages*
- *Braille books and magazines* - Cost that exceeds the regular printed edition of the book or magazine.
- *Breast reconstruction surgery* - Including breast prosthesis, following a mastectomy for cancer.
- *Capital Expenses* - You can include in medical expenses amounts you pay for special equipment installed in a home, or for improvements, if their main purpose is medical care for you, your spouse, or your dependent. The cost of permanent improvements that increase the value of your property may be partly included as a medical expense. The cost of the improvement is reduced by the increase in the value of your property. The difference is a medical expense. If the value of your property is not increased by the improvement, the entire cost is included as a medical expense.
- *Cars* - The cost of special hand controls and other special equipment installed for the use of a disabled person.
- *Chiropractor*
- *Christian Science practitioner*
- *Crutches*
- *Diagnostic devices* - Cost of devices used in diagnosing and treating illness and disease, such as a blood sugar test kit for a diabetic, even without a prescription.
- *Disabled dependent care expenses*
- *Eye Surgery* - You can include in medical expenses the amount you pay for eye surgery to treat defective vision, such as laser eye surgery or radial keratotomy.
- *Fertility enhancement* – Cost paid for procedures such as in vitro fertilization and surgery to reverse prior surgery that prevented the person from having children.
- *Guide dog or other service animal* - Cost of buying, training, and maintaining a guide dog or service animal to

assist a visually impaired or hearing disabled person, or a person with other physical disabilities.

- *Hearing Aids* - You can include in medical expenses the cost of a hearing aid and batteries, repairs, and maintenance needed to operate it.
- *Hospital Services* – You can include in medical expenses amounts you pay for the cost of inpatient care at a hospital or similar institution if a principal reason for being there is to receive medical care. This includes amounts paid for meals and lodging.
- *Long-term care insurance premiums*
- *Lead-based paint removal* - The cost of removing (but not the cost of repainting) lead-based paints from surfaces in the home to prevent a child who has or had lead poisoning from eating the paint. If, instead of removing the paint, the area is covered with wallboard or paneling, treat these as capital expenses.
- *Legal fees* - Legal fees paid to authorize treatment for mental illness.
- *Lifetime care (advance payments)* - You can include in medical expenses a part of a life-care fee or "founder's fee" you pay either monthly or as a lump sum under an agreement with a retirement home. The part of the payment you include is the amount properly allocable to medical care. The agreement must require that you pay a specific fee as a condition for the home's promise to provide lifetime care that includes medical care.
- *Medical conferences* - Admission and transportation to a medical conference if the conference concerns the chronic illness of the taxpayer, spouse, or dependent.
- *Medicare Part A, Part B, and Part D*
- *Nursing Home* - You can include in medical expenses the cost of medical care in a nursing home, home for the aged, or similar institution, for yourself, your spouse, or your dependents. This includes the cost of meals and lodging in the home if a principal reason for being there is to get

medical care.

- **Nursing Services** – You can include in medical expenses wages and other amounts you pay for nursing services. The services need not be performed by a nurse as long as the services are of a kind generally performed by a nurse. This includes services connected with caring for the patient's condition, such as giving medication or changing dressings, as well as bathing and grooming the patient. These services can be provided in your home or another care facility. Generally, only the amount spent for nursing services is a medical expense. If the attendant also provides personal and household services, amounts paid to the attendant must be divided between the time spent performing household and personal services and the time spent for nursing services.
- **Osteopath**
- **Psychoanalysis**
- **Telephone** – The cost of special telephone equipment for the hearing impaired, including repair costs.
- **Transplants**
- **Veterinary fees** – Only if incurred to maintain the health of a guide dog or other service animal so that it may perform its duties assisting a person with physical disabilities.
- **Weight-loss programs** – Are deductible medical expenses if they are a treatment for a specific disease diagnosed by a physician.
- **Wheelchair**
- **Wig** – You can include in medical expenses the cost of a wig purchased upon the advice of a physician for the mental health of a patient who has lost all of his or her hair from disease.

For a comprehensive list of deductible expenses, please refer to IRS Publication 502, *Medical and Dental Expenses.*

Jared R. Rogers, CPA

State and local taxes
The TCJA limited the itemized deduction for state and local taxes paid, including income taxes (or general sales taxes, if elected instead of income taxes), real estate taxes, and personal property taxes, to $10,000 ($5,000 MFS) through 2025. However, there are several types of taxes that can easily get one to the limitation. These include:

- State withholding reported on Forms W-2, W-2G, 1099-G, 1099-R, and 1099-MISC.
- Taxes paid in the tax year you are filing that were for a prior year balance due
- State and local estimated tax payments made
- Mandatory contributions made to:
  o The California, New Jersey, or New York Nonoccupational Disability Benefit Fund, Rhode Island Temporary Disability Benefit Fund, or Washington State Supplemental Workmen's Compensation Fund.
  o The Alaska, California, New Jersey, or Pennsylvania state unemployment fund.
  o State family leave programs, such as the New Jersey Family Leave Insurance (FLI) program and the California Paid Family Leave program.
- Real estate taxes paid
- Personal property taxes (if based on value alone and are charged on a yearly basis)

Home mortgage interest and points
Home mortgage interest is any interest paid on a loan secured by the taxpayer's qualified home. The loan may be a mortgage on the original purchase, a second mortgage, line of credit, or a home equity loan. To deduct interest paid, the taxpayer must be legally liable for the debt. A true debtor-creditor relationship must exist. The deductible amount depends on the date of the mortgage, the amount of the

mortgage, and how the taxpayer uses the proceeds. The biggest things to note is that the TCJA:

- limited the deductible amount of combined acquisition debt on main and second homes to $1 million ($500,000 MFS);
- suspended the deduction of home equity loan (i.e. HELOC) interest unless the loan proceeds were used to buy, build, or improve the home that secures the loan.

Charitable donations

Being charitable has many benefits; one of which is a deduction from Uncle Sam. To be deductible, a taxpayer must make charitable contributions to qualified organizations. Contributions to individuals are never deductible. If you receive a benefit from the contribution such as merchandise, goods or services, including admission to a charity ball, banquet, theatrical performance, or sporting event, you can only deduct the amount that exceeds the fair market value of the benefit received. To ensure that the deductions are not disallowed in the event of an audit, make note of the following documentation requirements:

- ***Contributions less than $250*** – Keep a copy of the bank record (e.g. check, bank statement, credit card statement), receipt, payroll record or pledge card.
- ***Contributions greater than $250*** – Get a written acknowledgement from the organization documenting this gift. This is needed even if you have a cancelled check as proof of the gift.
- ***Donated property valued at greater than $5,000*** – You must obtain a qualified written appraisal of the property.

Listed below are some things that many people fail to keep in mind or do as it relates to their donations:

- The total deduction for all charitable contributions is limited to 60 percent of the taxpayer's AGI. Contributions in excess of 60 percent of AGI are carried over to the next tax year. If your contributions were limited in one year, make sure they are taken in the subsequent year.
- Special rules apply for determining the value of used motor vehicles, boats, and airplanes. Your deduction is generally equal to the fair market value at the time of the donation. However, the deduction may be less than the FMV under the gross proceeds deduction limit.
- Most charities will use Form 1098-C to fulfill the written acknowledgement requirement for vehicles and the like. Make sure you attach Copy B to the donor's tax return or the IRS can disallow the deduction.

Casualty and theft losses

Generally, you may deduct casualty and theft losses relating to your home, household items, and vehicles on your federal income tax return if incurred within a federally declared disaster area by the President. You may not deduct casualty and theft losses covered by insurance unless you file a timely claim for reimbursement and you reduce the loss by the amount of any reimbursement or expected reimbursement.

A federally declared disaster is a disaster that occurred in an area declared by the President to be eligible for federal assistance under the Robert T. Stafford Disaster Relief and Emergency Assistance Act. It includes a major disaster or emergency declaration under the Act. A casualty loss can result from the damage, destruction, or loss of your property from any sudden, unexpected, or unusual event such as a flood, hurricane, tornado, fire, earthquake, or volcanic eruption. A casualty does not include normal wear and tear or progressive deterioration.

A theft is the taking and removal of money or property with the intent to deprive the owner of it. The taking must be illegal under the law of the state where it occurred and must have been done with criminal intent. The amount of your theft loss is generally the adjusted basis of your property because the fair market value of your property immediately after the theft is considered to be zero.

Author's note: While it is NOT a broker's job to render tax advice, it is helpful for you to know the basics I discussed above. One of the best things you can take away from the above is who is most likely to itemize so that you can sprinkle the tidbits you learned into the sales pitch. You know that all state and local taxes are capped at $10,000. So, if a taxpayer were to maximize that deduction, then the following gaps would still exist between the standard deduction and itemizing:

- $2,400 - Single and Married Filing Separately
- $14,800 - Married Filing Jointly and Surviving Spouses
- $8,650 – Head of Household

As you can gather, the lower the standard deduction, the greater the probability that one may be able to itemize their deductions. Why? Because it only takes a small dollar amount of the other items to get over the threshold. But for those that are married and file together, they would need more than $14,800 in combined mortgage interest, charitable deductions, and medical expenses to exceed the standard. So, unless you have a really expensive mortgage or are really charitable, the probability that you will be able to itemize begins to shrink pretty quickly.

SUMMARY
- As a broker, your job is not taxes. However, you can be an educator to your clients with regard to this topic when they are making a home purchase.
- When you file your tax return, you usually have a choice whether to take the standard deduction or itemize.
- The IRS will allow you to use whatever method yields

you the biggest benefit for that tax year.
- The standard deduction is determined based on your filing status.
- If the total allowable amounts spent on the following exceed that of the standard deduction, then a taxpayer will (and should) itemize:
  o Medical and dental expenses that exceed 7.5 percent of your AGI
  o State and local income or sales taxes
  o Real estate taxes
  o Personal property taxes
  o Mortgage interest and points
  o Investment interest
  o Gifts to charity
  o Disaster losses from a Federally declared disaster

NOTES

[1] 26 U.S. Code § 63. Taxable income defined. Available online at https://www.law.cornell.edu/uscode/text/26/63. (Accessed January 11, 2020).

[2] 26 U.S. Code § 63(C)(2). Taxable income defined; Basic standard deduction.

[3] 26 U.S. Code § 63(C)(3). Taxable income defined; Additional standard deduction for aged and blind

CHAPTER 6
Benefits for Landlords

Rental properties are probably one of the most common forms of "investment" property in the United States. This is because it allows the landlord to own the property and then have the tenants pay for substantially all the costs of ownership. If you are the owner of a rental property (i.e. landlord), there are numerous expenses the IRS will allow you to deduct on your tax return. Unfortunately, many people fail to properly track or include what they are allowed. Here, I will discuss some of the common deductions as well as the more commonly missed items.

What a landlord can deduct that a normal homeowner cannot

Rental properties have their own little set of rules. As I mentioned at the start of the book, even though I had passed the CPA exam, I had to learn all these rules when I purchased my first property. It is advisable that a broker learn these rules as well, because your clients will have questions. When you can speak to the rules in the language that investors deal and talk in, it can only aid you in getting a deal to close.

Come tax time, all landlords will report the income and expenses associated with their rental property on IRS Schedule E, *Supplemental Income and Loss*. If the property is owned by a S-Corp, Multimember LLC or partnership, then the activity is reported on IRS Form 8825, *Rental Real Estate Income and Expenses of a Partnership or an S-*Corporation. The income part is usually the simplest piece; just report the amount of income earned. However, it is the expense side that usually trips people up. Why?

Well, there are all these little nuanced rules surrounding rental activities. So, without knowledge of them, one may be confused when they enter an amount in their tax software but see a different or reduced amount on the tax return. This can happen when a property is used personally for more than 14 days per year or if an owner occupies a unit in a multifamily building. Notwithstanding the above, what can a landlord deduct? Here are the most often deducted expenses:

- Advertising
- Auto and travel expenses
- Cleaning and maintenance
- Commissions
- Insurance
- Legal and professional fees
- Management fees
- HOA fees (e.g. with respect to condos rented out)
- Mortgage interest
- Repairs
- Supplies
- Taxes
- Utilities
- Depreciation

Author's note: A landlord can deduct the amounts paid for repairs and maintenance. However, one cannot deduct the cost of improvements. Repair and maintenance costs are those expenses that keep the property in an ordinarily efficient operating condition. Examples are fixing a broken lock or painting a room.

In contrast, improvements are amounts paid to better or restore the property or adapt it to a new or different use. Examples of improvements are adding substantial insulation or replacing an entire HVAC system. Amounts paid to improve a property generally must be capitalized and depreciated (that is, they cannot be deducted in full in the year they are paid or incurred).

What a landlord needs to equally pay attention to are those

expenses which are allowed but occasionally missed. What am I talking about?

- **Expenses paid via cash** – Many property owners must pay for things like repairs, supplies, handyman work, and other things. But if they pay for them and do not get a receipt, it is almost certain that they will forget to include these costs on their return. Simple solution? Always get a receipt or carry a receipt book when engaging with those who do work on the property.

- **Other interest** – Include the amount of interest paid to third parties such as private investors, private businesses, crowdfunding platforms, or relatives. Also, make sure that these people or parties are sent a Form 1099-INT showing the interest that was paid to them. Without a Form 1099 it may be harder to substantiate the deduction if requested to do so by the IRS.

- **Management fees** – Include the cost to hire an agent or property manager to manage the rental. This may also include special service calls that the property manager incurs to check on the rental.

- **Office expenses** – Practically everything that is used in a landlord's office is considered a business expense. Some common expenses include printer ink, paper, pens, computer software, stationery, and envelopes.

- **Operating expense carryover** – If a landlord has a multiunit property where they rent some units but also live in one, then their deductible expenses cannot exceed their income. But these expenses are not lost, they are simply suspended and carried forward to future years. So, if in a following year they have more income than expenses, they can use these suspended expenses to offset their remaining income.

- **Suspended passive activity losses** – Rental activities are classified as passive. As such, their losses are limited on a taxpayer's income tax return based upon certain AGI amounts. Similar to above, they can become suspended but are carried forward to future years. If the taxpayer's income dips below certain levels in future years, then these losses can be released to offset current year income.

- *Other expenses* – Examples of these expenses may include postage, bank fees, education, subscriptions, cost of books, meals and entertainment, and gifts to clients or tenants. All of these "other" expenses are collectively itemized on a separate "supporting" page of the landlord's tax return. As some of the above deductions are bound by certain qualifications, make sure you consult with your tax professional.

Special $25,000 allowance for rental real estate

While no one wants to lose money as it relates to their rental property efforts, many of the aforementioned expenses often do generate a loss. Well, from a "paper" standpoint, that is! This section will discuss a special allowance granted by the IRS and some of the intricacies of claiming it.

If a taxpayer or spouse actively participates in a passive rental real estate activity, a loss deduction of up to $25,000 is allowed against non-passive income. Of course, certain requirements must be met as well. Yet, through proper planning, one can make sure that they maximize their ability to take this loss. Qualifications for the special $25,000 allowance are as follows:

- Actively participate in and own 10 percent or greater of the rental real estate activity.
- Have modified AGI of less than $100,000 ($50,000 if married filing separately).
- If modified AGI is greater than $150,000 ($75,000 married filing separately) then the allowance is completely phased out.

Some important nuances of the allowance are as follows:

- Active participation standards (not the same as material participation) are met if the taxpayer (or the taxpayer's spouse) participates in the management of the rental property in a significant and bona fide sense.
- The special allowance is reduced by 50 percent of the amount of modified AGI that is more than $100,000 ($50,000 MFS).
- If a taxpayer is married, files a separate return, and lived apart from the spouse for the entire tax year, the special allowance cannot be more than $12,500.
- If the taxpayer is married, filing a separate return, and lived with the spouse at any time during the year, the special allowance is not allowed.

If the qualifications are met, a landlord should ensure that either they or their tax professional deduct any allowed losses on their tax return. Furthermore, if they meet the real estate professional qualifications as previously discussed, then know that the losses are not capped at $25,000.

When a rental property is classified as a trade or business

It is to landlord's advantage tax-wise to categorize their rental activities as a business, not an investment. As mentioned in Chapter 2, the TCJA created a new 20 percent deduction for those with QBI. To be eligible, one must have QBI from a "qualified" trade or business. The bothersome question in the whole year that followed §199A being enacted was if and when a rental activity was considered a trade or business. The Supreme Court held in *Commissioner v. Groetzinger*[1] that an activity rises to the level of a trade or business if it is engaged in continuously and regularly for the purpose of making a profit. However, this was a very broad standard, and the facts did not involve rental real estate. As such, applying this rather vague test was often a highly factual and individualized determination and really did not lend itself to the whole QBI situation nicely.

When the QBI regulations were issued, the IRS stated[2] that the relevant factors to be considered for rental real estate included, but were not limited to:

- the type of rented property (commercial versus residential property)
- the number of properties rented
- the owner's or the owner's agent's day-to-day involvement
- the types and significance of any ancillary services provided under the lease
- the terms of the lease (for example, a short-term versus long-term lease), and
- whether the landlord has filed all required information returns.

Yet, with all the above, taxpayers could still find it unclear if "their" rental activity qualified them to take the deduction. So, in 2019, the IRS devised and released a safe harbor for taxpayers to utilize.

For purposes of the QBI deduction, landlords who satisfy the rule's requirements are automatically deemed to be "in business" for purpose of the deduction, but for no other purpose. To qualify to use the safe harbor a landlord must:[3]

- perform a total of 250 hours of real estate rental services each year (including work performed by employees and agents)
- keep records documenting the real estate services performed, and
- keep separate books and records showing income and expenses for each rental real estate enterprise.

Use of this safe harbor rule is purely optional. A landlord does not need it if their rental activity qualifies as a business under the regular rules covered above. Also, the safe harbor cannot be used by landlords who use the property involved as a residence more than 14 days during the year, which eliminates most short-term rental hosts.

Author's note: A careful and detailed analysis of the facts is necessary when determining whether a rental activity is a trade or business. However, this analysis can provide significant benefits as the prize for achieving trade or business status is avoidance of the Net Investment Income Tax (assuming the landlord is also non-passive) and potential eligibility for the 20 percent QBI deduction. Additional benefits could include qualifying for Section 1231 treatment (with regards to losses and gains) as well as writing off home office expenses associated with managing the rental activity.

SUMMARY

- If you are the owner of a rental property (i.e. landlord), there are numerous expenses the IRS will allow you to deduct on your tax return.
- A landlord can deduct the amounts paid for repairs and maintenance. However, they cannot deduct the cost of improvements.
- Amounts paid to improve the property generally must be capitalized and depreciated (that is, they cannot be deducted in full in the year they are paid or incurred).
- What a landlord needs to equally pay attention to, are those expenses which are allowed, but occasionally missed.
- If a taxpayer, or spouse, actively participates in a passive rental real estate activity, a loss deduction of up to $25,000 is allowed against non-passive income.
- If a person meets the real estate professional qualifications as previously discussed, then know that their losses are not capped at $25,000.
- If one has QBI from a qualified trade or business, their

rental property may qualify them to take the 20 percent deduction.

- For purposes of the QBI deduction, landlords who satisfy the safe harbor rule's requirements are automatically deemed to be "in business" for purpose of the deduction, but for no other purpose.

NOTES

[1] *Commissioner v. Groetzinger* 480 U.S. 23 (1987).

[2] Preamble to IRS Reg. 1.199A-1.

[3] Department of the Treasury, Internal Revenue Service, Notice 2019-7, (Washington, DC: 2019), https://www.irs.gov/pub/irs-drop/n-19-07.pdf

CHAPTER 7
Tax Implications of Property Disposal

One thing that is almost as certain as the sun rising every day is that when a person sells something at a gain, Uncle Sam wants his cut! Yet some of the biggest tax misunderstandings regarding real estate surround capital gains. In certain instances, one can sell a property and pay no tax on the gain. In other instances, one can potentially take the gain and defer it. Lastly, a property owner simply may be on the hook for the taxes with no way to avoid them. In this chapter, I will discuss the various tax implications of property disposals.

Excluding the gain on the sale of a principal residence

If a person has owned his or her home for any length of time, it is quite possible that it has appreciated in value. To that end, when they sell it to the buyer, the sale may generate a taxable gain. However, if this was the seller's principal residence, there is the possibility that the gain may be excludable from their taxable income. How you may ask? Via the Principal Residence Gain Exclusion.

The general rule is that a taxpayer may exclude up to $250,000 of gain from the sale of their principal residence ($500,000 if married filing jointly) if they meet the following requirements:[1]

- If they have owned the residence for any two of the last five years.
- If they have occupied the residence for any two of the last five years.
- If they have not used the exclusion within the last two years.

Example: Darnell is a single taxpayer who owns his own home. He has lived in the home since he purchased it in 2014 and has made some improvements to it. In 2019 because he got engaged, he decides to sell his home and purchase a new one with his fiancé. He sells his home at a gain but is not sure if he will have to pay taxes on it. Come tax time, the calculations in **Figure 7-1** are performed to determine the answer to his question:

May 5, 2014 purchased home for	$175,000
September 10, 2014 homeowner paid for renovations	$47,000
Homeowner's basis:	**$222,000**
July 4, 2019 sold home for	$385,000
Homeowner's basis	$222,000
Potential gain on sale:	**$163,000**
Maximum gain exclusion for single filing status	$250,000
Gain on sale	$163,000
Remaining gain exclusion:	**$87,000**

Figure 7-1

So, as you can see in this instance, the homeowner was able to exclude his $163,000 gain from taxes. Furthermore, he could have sold his home for an additional $87,000 before any of the gain would have been taxable.

Author's note: The one thing I want to highlight is that a taxpayer must not have used the exclusion within the last two years. However, this exclusion can be used repeatedly. So, if a person has a principal residence, sells it, and uses the exclusion, then buys another home as his principal residence, it is possible that he can use the exclusion again if he sells the second home. The key point is that he must make that home his principal residence. From there, he must live in it for two years leading up to the five-year period ending with the sale date, sell the home, and then take the exclusion.

From time to time, I will have taxpayers come to me with one of two scenarios. The first is that they sold their home but did not own it for 5 years. Can they still get the exclusion? The second one typically involves a home that was converted to a rental property (or had home office use) where depreciation was taken. Can they take the exclusion and if so, what about the depreciation? As with all things tax, the answer can vary depending on the circumstances. So, let us examine each scenario a little closer, shall we?

Let us assume that a homeowner must sell her home. She owned it for four years and it was her principal residence for that entire period. In this case, she did not own it for five years. However, per the IRS:[2]

"If you do not meet the Eligibility Test, you may still qualify for a partial exclusion of gain. You can meet the requirements for a partial exclusion if the main reason for your home sale was a change in workplace location, a health issue, or an unforeseeable event."

What the above means is that all is not lost if a taxpayer has to sell her home when she did not own it for five years. She would just have to see if she meets at least one of the exceptions. IRS Publication 523, *Selling Your Home,* lists what qualifies under each exception. Let us look at another brief example.

Example: Marco's Multiple Sclerosis symptoms became unbearable. He was advised by his doctor to move to a cooler climate to manage his symptoms better. He had only owned his home a little over one year prior to having to sell it. **Figure 7-2** illustrates the facts surrounding the sale of his home as well as the calculations involved in the partial gain exclusion. What we can see is that even though he did not use the home for two out of five years, he is allowed a partial exclusion. The result is that he can exclude the $85,000 gain on the sale of his home, and he could have sold it for another $60,205 before his gain would have been taxable.

June 1, 2018 purchased home for	$280,000
July 30, 2019 sold home for	$365,000
Potential gain on sale:	**$85,000**

Time of residency in and ownership of home (in days)	424
Two year exclusion period (in days)	730
Exclusion Percentage	58%
Maximum gain exclusion for single filing status	$250,000
Partial gain exclusion allowed:	**$145,205**

Partial gain exclusion allowed	$145,205
Gain on sale	$85,000
Remaining gain exclusion:	**$60,205**

Figure 7-2

Now, what about that depreciation question? I will not bore you with all the technical tax aspects that go into this scenario. In summary, per the IRS:[3]

"If you used all or part of your home for business or rental after May 6, 1997, you may need to pay back ("recapture") some or all of the depreciation you were entitled to take on your property. "Recapturing" depreciation means you must include it as ordinary income on your tax return."

What this means is that if a taxpayer took depreciation, a portion of the gain (up to the amount taken as depreciation) may be taxed up to a maximum special long-term capital gain rate of 25 percent. I will discuss this more in a moment. Yet, the key takeaway is that if you or a client are facing this scenario, it is best to seek the expertise of an experienced and qualified tax advisor.

Understanding Cancellation of Debt Income
When the real estate market crashed back in 2008, it caused a lot of financial heartache for those who had purchased

at the market's height. In the years that followed, some homeowners, investors, and landlords simply could not keep up with making their mortgage or loan payments. In some instances, people chose to simply let the property go into foreclosure or just abandoned it altogether. Well, from the IRS' perspective, either of the two scenarios constitutes a "disposal" of the property similar to a "normal" sale. This means that one has to calculate and potentially report a gain or a loss on that sale on their tax return. What is worse, if debt is cancelled (i.e. forgiven) in the process, one may also have to account for cancellation of debt income.

You see, if someone borrows money and is legally obligated to repay it at a future date, they have a debt. They may be personally liable for the debt or may own a property that is subject to the debt. If that debt is forgiven or discharged for less than the full amount they owe, the debt is considered canceled in the amount that they do not have to pay. This canceled amount generally has to be included in income and reported on that year's tax return. However, the law provides several exceptions in which the canceled debt can be excluded from taxable income.

There are five instances in which canceled debt is excludable from taxable income. They include:[4]

- Debt canceled in a Title 11 bankruptcy case
- Debt canceled during insolvency
- Cancellation of qualified farm indebtedness
- Cancellation of qualified real property business indebtedness
- Cancellation of qualified principal residence indebtedness

The instances that will matter the most to a broker are the last two. These represent landlords and homeowners respectively. To that end, these taxpayers can exclude the cancellation of debt income if the associated property meets the respective

Jared R. Rogers, CPA

definition. If a taxpayer excludes cancelled debt from income, he or she must report it to the IRS. This is done by using IRS Form 982, *Reduction of Tax Attributes Due to Discharge of Indebtedness.*

So, as a broker, you now know that just because a taxpayer has debt cancelled, it does not automatically mean that it will have to be included in one's taxable income. People should do their due diligence and seek out help if needed. If they can exclude the income and are entitled to do so, they should.

Sale of rental property and depreciation recapture

As I mentioned earlier, if a taxpayer took depreciation on a property on their income tax return, the gain could be taxed at 25 percent when they sell it. The term "depreciation recapture" refers to the amount of gain that is treated as ordinary income upon the sale or other disposition of property. Gain that is treated as capital gain is not depreciation recapture.

Example: Larry Landlord bought a rental property in 2010 for $200,000. In 2019, he managed to sell it for $175,000. If life was simple, he could get away with the following calculation: his loss is the $175,000 sales prices less the $200,000 purchase price, or $25,000. He held the property more than a year, therefore it is a "long-term" loss. Done, right? Not so fast, my friend!

Unfortunately, it is not so simple, and instead of having a loss, Larry actually has had a gain. How come? Because of depreciation. Every year since 2010, he was depreciating the property, correct? Well, that depreciation lowered his tax bill and he received a benefit because of it. But if he thinks he got a free ride from the government, think again. What he was saving on depreciation comes back to haunt him when he sells the property.

So, for simplicity, let us assume that each year he received

$7,272 in depreciation ($200,000 purchase price/27.5 year useful life). This is approximately $73,000 of depreciation over the 10 years. Thus, the building was not really worth $200,000 for tax purposes, but only $127,000. Since he sold the building for $175,000, he really had a $48,000 gain!

It gets worse. The portion of any unrecaptured Section 1250 gain from selling Section 1250 real property is taxed at a maximum 25 percent rate. The actual calculations can get quite involved depending on the amount of the gain, the amount of depreciation taken, and the tax bracket you fall into. But once again for simplicity (and illustration), since he took $73,000 of depreciation, the entire $48,000 gain would be considered depreciation recapture, and he could pay $12,000 in taxes related to it. IRS Publication 544, *Sales and Other Dispositions of Assets,* offers a more detailed discussion on depreciation recapture if you are really interested.

Author's note: Selling certain types of property can result in significant tax consequences. Yet, proper tax planning can help a taxpayer deal with them, so they do not become tax problems. The key thing to do is speak to a tax professional prior to disposing of property that one believes may be subject to depreciation recapture. They can help the person forecast the associated tax implications so that they can set aside some of the proceeds of the sale (if needed) to address any related tax liabilities.

SUMMARY

- When a property is sold at a gain, be it a principal residence, investment property, or rental property, Uncle Sam usually wants his cut!
- There are several instances in which one might be able to exclude the gain of various types of income (e.g. capital gains, cancellation of debt income, etc.).
- The Principal Residence Gain Exclusion allows a taxpayer to exclude up to $250,000 of gain from the sale of their

principal residence ($500,000 if married filing jointly) if they meet certain requirements.

- The Principal Residence Gain Exclusion can be used repeatedly, and may be able to be used on each and every home a taxpayer sells if certain circumstances are met.

- If one does not meet the eligibility test to exclude their entire gain, they may still qualify for a partial exclusion of gain.

- One can meet the requirements for a partial exclusion if the main reason for the home sale was a change in workplace location, a health issue, or an unforeseeable event.

- If a taxpayer used all or part of their home for business or rental after May 6, 1997, they may need to pay back ("recapture") some or all of the depreciation they were entitled to take on their property.

- If one's debt is forgiven or discharged for less than the full amount they owe, the debt is considered canceled in the amount that they do not have to pay. This canceled amount generally has to be included in income and reported on their tax return.

- The law provides several exceptions in which the canceled debt can be excluded from one's taxable income.

NOTES

[1] 26 U.S. Code § 121. Exclusion of gain from sale of principal residence. Available online at https://www.law.cornell.edu/uscode/text/26/121. (Accessed January 11, 2020).

[2] Department of the Treasury, Internal Revenue Service, Publication 523, *Selling Your Home* (Washington, DC: 2018), https://www.irs.gov/pub/irs-pdf/p523.pdf.

[3] Ibid.

[4] 26 U.S. Code § 108(a). Income from discharge of indebtedness; Exclusion from gross income. Available online at https://www.law.cornell.edu/uscode/text/26/108. (Accessed January 11, 2020).

CHAPTER 8
Delaying Taxation

Selling a property for a huge profit is nearly every property owner's dream come true. Who would not want to make a pretty penny off his or her home? However, as we have learned, there are often tax consequences when one profits from a sale. Yet, what if a person could defer taking the profit as a lump sum? In doing so, they could spread out paying the associated tax liability, right? In this chapter, I will discuss some of the options available to do just that.

The Section 1031 Exchange

Most real estate investors have at least heard of the 1031 exchange, but very few have actually completed such a transaction. The 1031 exchange is a powerful tool to have in your creative real estate arsenal, as it allows people to dispose of one property and acquire another without paying capital gains tax on the property being disposed of. However, a 1031 exchange requires careful attention to the requirements, particularly as they relate to timing, in order to avoid potentially ghoulish dealings with the IRS.

To start with, it is important to understand exactly what a 1031 exchange is. Named after the section of the Internal Revenue Code under which it resides, a 1031 exchange is the swap of one asset for another similar asset. In other words, in order to take advantage of this tax section, the type of property swapped must be of a similar "nature or character." Fortunately, this is not much of an issue with real estate, as the code allows for the exchange of any real property for any other real property.

As a result of the TCJA, effective January 1, 2018, like-kind exchange treatment only applies to real property that is held for use in a trade or business or for investment. Real property, more commonly referred to as real estate, includes land and anything built on or attached to the land. Under the new law, the prior tax-deferral benefit of gains no longer applies to the following personal and other property:

- Machinery
- Equipment
- Vehicles
- Artwork/Collectibles
- Patents/Other Intellectual Property

Real property held primarily for sale (i.e. inventory) and real estate property located outside of the United States also does not qualify for like-kind exchange treatment; this rule remains unchanged from prior tax law. Lastly, personal residences are not eligible for like-kind exchanges; the property must have been an investment or business property to qualify. Now, let us go into some of the finer points involved in the process, which are depicted in **Figure 8-1**.

One of the nicest features of the rule is that the properties do not have to be of similar "grade or quality." In other words, it is perfectly legitimate to exchange a rental property in much need of repairs for a property that is in pristine condition. The like-kind exchange is an ideal vehicle for trading up properties without paying capital gains taxes. Timing is a key element to a successful 1031 exchange. In order to qualify for the capital gains deferral, the decision to treat a property sale as part of a 1031 exchange needs to be made <u>before</u> the closing date of the sale of that property. Then, the seller must identify the property to be acquired in the exchange within 45 days of the closing date of the sold property. The new property must then be acquired within 180 days of the date that the prior property was sold.

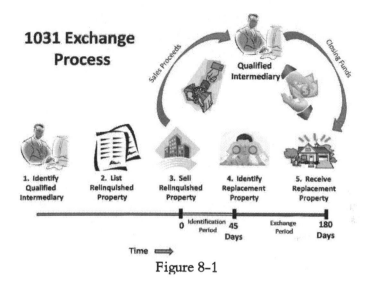

Figure 8-1

When it comes to identifying the replacement property, there are some interesting rules, and one can pick the rule they want to follow. The property needs to be of equal or greater value, but one can select multiple properties as potential properties to buy, subject to the following rules:[1]

1. You can select up to three distinct properties as possible replacement properties for the exchange, regardless of their value, OR…

2. You can select any number of properties, as long as their total fair market value does not exceed double the value of the property you sold, OR…

3. You can select any number of potential properties to buy, as long as the fair market value of the property you eventually close on within the 180-day window is at least 95 percent of the value of the property you sold.

In order to protect the "integrity" of the like-kind exchange, the IRS requires that the seller use a qualified intermediary in order to complete the transaction and qualify for the capital gains exclusion. These individuals are sometimes also referred to as "exchange accommodators" or "1031 exchange facilitators." The qualified intermediary escrows the proceeds from the sale of the first property and ensures that the funds are only used to acquire a like-kind property.

The qualified intermediary works with the title company, escrow company, or closing attorney to facilitate the transaction. The key element of this part of the transaction is to ensure that the seller never actually obtains receipt of the funds from the property sold, and there is no record of it passing through their personal accounts. Below is a warning from the IRS regarding this that is so well written, it is being included verbatim:[2]

"It is important to know that taking control of cash or other proceeds before the exchange is complete may disqualify the entire transaction from like-kind exchange treatment and make ALL gain immediately taxable.

If cash or other proceeds that are not like-kind property are received at the conclusion of the exchange, the transaction will still qualify as a like-kind exchange. Gain may be taxable, but only to the extent of the proceeds that are not like-kind property.

One way to avoid premature receipt of cash or other proceeds is to use a qualified intermediary or other exchange facilitator to hold those proceeds until the exchange is complete.

You cannot act as your own facilitator. In addition, your agent (including your real estate agent or broker, investment banker or broker, accountant, attorney, employee or anyone who has worked for you in those capacities within the previous two years) cannot act as your facilitator.

Be careful in your selection of a qualified intermediary as there have been recent incidents of intermediaries declaring bankruptcy or otherwise being unable to meet their contractual obligations to the taxpayer. These situations have resulted in taxpayers not meeting the strict timelines set for a deferred or reverse exchange, thereby disqualifying the transaction from Section 1031 deferral of gain. The gain may be taxable in the current year while any losses the taxpayer suffered would be considered under separate code sections."

Normally when an investment property is sold, a taxpayer must recapture the sum total of the depreciation they have claimed on the property. In other words, their taxable capital gains include not only the actual appreciation in the property's value, but also the amount that they deducted as depreciation over the time they owned the property. A beautiful benefit of the 1031 exchange is that there is no depreciation recapture required. Instead, the accumulated depreciation in the old property affects one's basis in the new property they are buying in the exchange.

Since the purpose of the like-kind exchange is to avoid paying capital gains tax on appreciation of properties, there is no benefit to using a 1031 exchange on a property on which the seller has a loss. By selling a property for a loss, a portion of that loss becomes deductible. The 1031 exchange rules do not recognize losses as an adjustment to the basis in the newly acquired property, so there is no benefit in using this vehicle for that purpose.

My hope is that the above has provided you with enough information so that you can help your clients (or yourself) make the decision of when to use the 1031 exchange rules. As with all things, however, make sure to consult with a licensed tax professional for advice regarding the specific transaction, and remember that a qualified intermediary must be used in order to complete the transaction.

Section 1033 Involuntary Conversions

For those brokers who work with clients near flood zones or tornado areas, this section is for you. So, pay attention! An involuntary conversion occurs when the owner's property is destroyed, stolen, condemned, or disposed of under the threat of condemnation and they receive other property or money in payment (such as insurance or a condemnation award). Involuntary conversions are also called involuntary exchanges. However, depending on the type of property received, the taxpayer may not have to report a gain on an involuntary conversion. For example, you do not report the gain if you receive property that is similar or related in service or use to the converted property.[3] Let us look at this a little more closely.

A conversion may be either direct, where a property is converted directly into similar property, or, more commonly, indirect, where property is converted into cash or dissimilar property.[4] The deferral of gain from a direct conversion is mandatory. However, the deferral of gain realized in an indirect conversion is elective and certain steps need to be taken in order to receive non-recognition treatment. A property is involuntarily converted when one of four events occurs:

1. The property is destroyed by fire, earthquake, hurricane, or some other destructive event.
2. The property is taken by theft (usually personal property).
3. The property is seized (generally without compensation, making this conversion somewhat irrelevant).
4. The requisition or condemnation of the property...
    (i) ..occurs through governmental exercise of its power of eminent domain. Must be compensable and involuntary.
    (ii) ..occurs through a sale due to an imminent threat of a

requisition or condemnation. The property owner must be aware of the threat and must reasonably believe that a condemnation is likely to occur.

The two most common indirect conversions are those by destruction, which is usually compensable through insurance payouts, and condemnations through eminent domain proceedings.

In order to defer the gain of an involuntary conversion, the taxpayer simply has to purchase replacement property within the replacement period. The election is made by attaching detailed statements to the tax returns in the year the gain is realized and in which the replacement property is acquired. What exactly is the replacement period? The replacement period starts from the earliest of:

1. the date the converted property is disposed of; or
2. the date of a threat or imminence of requisition or condemnation.

As such, the replacement period ends anywhere from two to four years from the end of the tax-year during which any part of the gain is realized.[5]

Example: Lisa Landlord had a $500,000 basis in a rental property that was destroyed in a tornado and she received a $600,000 settlement from the insurance company. Under Internal Revenue Code Section 1033, she has up to three years to invest those funds into a replacement property and avoid having to report a gain on the $100,000. However, if she were to invest less than the $600,000 in a replacement property, the amount of cash that she kept or otherwise spent would be considered a gain that would have to be reported.

Installment sales
An installment sale is the sale of property where the seller

receives at least one payment after the tax year of the sale. If a gain is realized on an installment sale, the seller may be able to report part of it when he or she receives each payment. This method of reporting the gain is called the "installment method." Essentially, this arrangement permits sellers to declare a prorated portion of their capital gain over several years, as long as the proper paperwork is completed during the year of the sale. So why is this advantageous?

When property is sold in this manner, the taxpayer must declare the gain each year as being long-term or short-term depending on whether the gain was long-term or short-term in the year of the sale. Long-term gains are taxed at a lower rate, while short-term gains are taxed as ordinary income. Since most rental properties are held for many years, they often involve long term gains. The capital gains rates for 2020 are either zero percent, 15 percent or 20 percent depending on the taxpayer's taxable income and the type of income. With that said, the real advantage of using the installment method boils down to:

- **Tax Deferral.** Instead of paying tax on the entire gain in one year, only a portion of the gain is taxable in the year of the sale. The remainder is taxable in the years payments are received. The taxable portion of each payment is based on the "gross profit ratio." To calculate this ratio, divide the gross profit from the sale by the price.
- **Lower tax liability.** Because the gain from an installment sale is spread out over several years, the seller may benefit from the tax rate differential in each of those years.

Example: Michael receives $600,000 for his rental home. He bought the property for $376,000 and paid $24,000 in selling expenses, which are added to the home's basis, making it $400,000. Therefore, Michael has $200,000 ($600,000 − $400,000) of reportable gain to declare. When Michael told his tax advisor about the sale, the advisor was less than excited;

taking the income as one lump sum would not be in Michael's best interest from a tax perspective. If he declares the entire proceeds of the sale in the same year he sells the property, he will be ineligible for virtually all of the tax credits to which he would normally be entitled.

Michael's advisor recommends he break down his sale proceeds into four annual installments of $50,000 each, instead of declaring $200,000 in one year. As long as the installments are constructively received each year, this method will allow Michael to remain eligible for tax credits and deductions that the lump-sum payment would have prevented him from receiving. To illustrate the tax impact, let us assume that the $50,000 annual gain is taxed at the 15 percent rate each year instead of the 20 percent rate (if the entire gain had been taxed in the year of sale). As a result, Michael saves $2,500 ($50,000 x 5 percent tax rate differential) each year for a total savings of $10,000 ($2,500 x 4 years). Furthermore, he gets to spread out the taxes he has to pay on the $200,000 gain over four years versus having to pay in all at once.

SUMMARY
- The 1031 exchange is a powerful tool to have in your creative real estate arsenal, as it allows one to dispose of a property and acquire another without paying capital gains tax on the property being disposing of.
- Like-kind exchange treatment only applies to real property that is held for use in a trade or business or for investment.
- Real property, more commonly referred to as real estate, includes land and anything built on or attached to the land.
- There are many fine points surrounding a 1031 exchange that must be considered such as timing or property disposal and acquisition, property identification, and the use of a qualified intermediary.
- In order to protect the "integrity" of the like-kind exchange, the IRS requires that the seller use a qualified intermediary in order to complete the transaction and

qualify for the capital gains exclusion.

- Since the purpose of the like-kind exchange is to avoid paying capital gains tax on appreciation of properties, there is no benefit to using a 1031 exchange on a property on which the seller has a loss.

- An involuntary conversion occurs when the owner's property is destroyed, stolen, condemned, or disposed of under the threat of condemnation and they receive other property or money in payment

- However, depending on the type of property received, the taxpayer may not have to report a gain on an involuntary conversion.

- An installment sale is the sale of property where the seller receives at least one payment after the tax year of the sale.

- Essentially, this arrangement permits sellers to declare a prorated portion of their capital gain over several years, as long as the proper paperwork is completed during the year of the sale.

NOTES

[1] Department of the Treasury, Internal Revenue Service, Publication 544, *Sales and Other Dispositions of Assets* (Washington, DC: 2019), https://www.irs.gov/pub/irs-pdf/p544.pdf

[2] Department of the Treasury, Internal Revenue Service, Fact Sheet 2008-18 *Like-Kind Exchanges Under IRC Section 1031,* (Washington, DC: 2008), https://www.irs.gov/pub/irs-news/fs-08-18.pdf.

[3] 26 U.S. Code § 1033(a)(1). Involuntary conversions; Conversion into similar property. Available online at https://www.law.cornell.edu/uscode/text/26/1033. (Accessed January 11, 2020).

[4] 26 U.S. Code §1033(a)(1) and (a)(2) respectively

[5] 26 U.S. Code §1033(a)(2)(b); 1033(g)(4); and 1033(h)(1)(b)

SECTION III
Dealing with Tax Problems –
Yours and Your Clients

CHAPTER 9
What to Do If YOU
Get in Trouble with the IRS

Real estate brokers and other self-employed individuals have a higher instance of tax compliance problems than those who simply get a W2 and have taxes withheld from their paychecks. Why? Well, a broker can see a lot of variation or fluctuation in their cash flow. They may work for months between sales with nothing but a lot of driving around, talking to prospects, and having meetings, none of which are paying the bills, right? Then a commission check comes in and the broker is not in a position to send 30 to 40 percent to the IRS and state taxing body. Sound familiar?

Some brokers take a stab at doing their own taxes using software. When they see the resulting balance, they get freaked out and never file it. They kind of try and forget about it and hope they can get everything caught up and filed before the IRS catches up with them. The next thing they know, two, three, or maybe four years pass, and they are wondering if they can ever get back on track. Well, I am here to reassure you that "yes" you can recover and get back into the tax system. In this chapter (which will probably be the longest), I am going to take you through all of the important information you need to know if you (or a broker you know) are facing tax problems.

Understanding what the IRS' job REALLY is
The IRS originated with the Commissioner of Internal Revenue, a Federal office created in 1862 to assess the nation's first income tax, which was to raise funds for the American Civil War. This measure provided over a fifth of the Union's war expenses, but was only temporary and allowed to expire a decade later. In 1913, the Sixteenth Amendment to the U.S. Constitution was ratified authorizing Congress to impose a tax on income, and the Bureau of Internal Revenue was

established. In 1953, the agency was renamed the Internal Revenue Service. The IRS is the revenue service of the U.S. government and is a bureau of the Department of the Treasury. Basically, the IRS is the debt collector and the Treasury is the bank!

The IRS is responsible for collecting taxes and administering the Internal Revenue Code, the main body of tax law in the U.S. Its duties include providing tax assistance to taxpayers and pursuing and resolving instances of erroneous or fraudulent tax filings. During Fiscal Year 2018, the IRS collected nearly $3.5 trillion, processed more than 250 million tax returns and other forms, and issued almost $464 billion in tax refunds.[1] The IRS' budget during this same period was $11.7 billion, resulting in $0.34 of taxpayer dollars being spent to collect every $100 in revenue.[2] A key difference in the U.S. tax system when compared to other countries, is that it is largely one of voluntary compliance. Meaning, it is up to the taxpayer to tell the government how much they earned and should be taxed as opposed to the other way around.

However, if the system was REALLY completely voluntary, how could the government guarantee that taxpayers paid their fair share? This is why the term "voluntary compliance" is a little misleading. As I mentioned, the IRS is the largest and most powerful collection agency. Furthermore, it does a good job or reminding folks that it can do things to you that no other debt collector can. Did you hear what happened to Wesley Snipes, Willie Nelson, Leona Helmsley, and Al Capone? Well, a lot of this is done on purpose to keep the sheep in line. This IRS likes it when people think "If they could do that to so-and-so, then what would they do to little 'ol me?"

Nasty things the IRS can do to you

The IRS has a few tools in its arsenal to get a person to comply with paying the taxes they owe. The ones people are most aware of are liens and levies. While a lien establishes that the government has a legal claim against a taxpayer, it is not what most taxpayers have to worry about. A levy, on the other hand, is something everyone should be afraid of. This is because it allows the IRS to seize property, cash, or wages. Below, I will explain what each item is and how it can impact you or a client who has tax problems.

<u>Liens</u>

As stated above, a lien gives the IRS claim to your property. It is their security towards ensuring that you pay the taxes owed to them. Your "property" essentially means any and everything that you own. This can include items such as your house, car, retirement accounts, social security payments, or your paycheck (yup, that is fair game, too). If you try to just "disappear" and get rid of your assets, you will quickly find that it will be next to impossible because of the lien. This is because once it is filed, it attaches to all your property. All your creditors will be notified of the tax lien, which means that if you sell your house, car, or other property, the IRS will be the first to get paid, not the creditor.

Section 6321 of the Internal Revenue Code states that:

"If any person liable to pay any tax neglects or refuses to pay the same after demand, the amount (including any interest, additional amount, addition to tax, or assessable penalty, together with any costs that may accrue in addition thereto) shall be a lien in favor of the United States upon all property and rights to property, whether real or personal, belonging to such person."

Now, the important thing to know about a lien is that the IRS just cannot file it at will. There are procedures that they must follow:

- The IRS must assess the liability (i.e. tax) against you.

- They must send you a Notice and Demand for Payment (essentially a bill that tells you how much you owe).
- You have ten days to pay the taxes owed after the IRS sends the above notice.
- If you fail to pay after the ten days, a tax lien will automatically be filed against you.

Paying your tax debt in full is the best way to get rid of a tax lien. Once you pay your debt (including any interest and other additions) the IRS will issue a Release of the Notice of Federal Tax Lien. This is supposed to be filed within thirty days of the tax debt being paid, however, it is not uncommon for it to not be done. Furthermore, even if they do file it, it can take months or years for the release to be picked up by credit reporting agencies.

Levies

A levy is the legal seizure of your property to satisfy a tax debt. Section 6331 of the Internal Revenue Code authorizes levies to collect delinquent tax. Similar to a lien, the IRS will usually only levy a taxpayer after certain requirements are met. These requirements are:

- The IRS assessed the tax and sent the taxpayer a Notice and Demand for Payment (a tax bill);
- The taxpayer neglected or refused to pay the tax; and
- The IRS sent the taxpayer a Final Notice of Intent to Levy and Notice of Your Right to A Hearing (IRS Letter 1058) at least 30 days before the levy. The IRS may give this notice in person, leave it at the taxpayers' home or usual place of business, or send it to their last known address by certified or registered mail, return receipt requested.

What causes the IRS to execute a levy? If taxpayers do not pay their taxes (or make arrangements to settle their debt), the IRS determines that a levy is the best action it has to collect on the taxes due. Note that the IRS could levy property that belongs to a taxpayer, but is held by someone else (such as their wages, retirement accounts, dividends, bank accounts, licenses, rental income, accounts receivables, the cash loan value of their life insurance, or commissions). Or, the IRS could seize and sell property that a taxpayer holds (such as their car, boat or house). Which brings us to our next topic.

<u>Seizures</u>

So how is a seizure different from a levy? It is no different, just merely a subset. You see, levies are normally divided into two categories. The first category includes tangible, real, and personal property that you own. The second includes third parties who hold property belonging to you such as bank deposits and wages. The first category is often referred to as a "seizure" while the second category is referred to as a "levy" or "garnishment."

A notice of seizure is the final document the government must produce in the process of seizing property for nonpayment of federal taxes. If the taxpayer ignores the Notice of Demand for Payment or fails to pay the debt in full, the IRS will ultimately send a letter indicating its intent to levy the individual taxpayer's or business's assets. At this point, all of their assets are at risk. When the IRS ultimately seizes the assets, it is required to leave a copy of the Notice of Seizure at the site of the seizure, and it is also required to mail copies by regular and certified mail to the relevant individual's last known address and workplace.

Once the IRS seizes a house or other property, they will arrange for it to be sold and apply the proceeds (after the costs of the sale) to the taxpayer's tax debt. Prior to selling their property, the IRS will calculate a minimum bid price. They will then provide the taxpayer with a copy of the calculation and give them an opportunity to challenge the fair market value determination. They will also provide the taxpayer with the notice of sale and announce the pending sale to the public, usually through local newspapers or flyers posted in public places. After giving public notice, the IRS will generally wait at least 10 days before selling the taxpayers' property. Money from the sale pays for the cost of seizing and selling the property and, finally, the taxpayer's tax debt. If there is money left over from the sale after paying off the tax debt, the IRS will tell the taxpayer how to get their refund.

Wage Garnishments

Simply put, a wage garnishment is when the IRS locates a debtor's employer and takes their wages during each pay period until the debt is paid in full. A wage garnishment can be used to collect a debt that a taxpayer owes due to a late filing. It can also be used when a person files their return correctly but does not pay the full balance of their debt. To implement the garnishment, the IRS obtains a judgment and sends it to the debtor's employer. The employer is then *required* to withhold a certain amount of the individual's paycheck each pay period and send it to the IRS until the debt has been fully paid. Depending on state laws, a garnishment may take anywhere from 30 percent to 70 percent of a person's paycheck to cover their unpaid debts!

Furthermore, the IRS is particularly tough. It can garnish a taxpayer's income and, if they are retired and collecting government benefits, it can also take their Social Security checks too! The levy usually is not lifted until the debt is paid off in full. However, a taxpayer does have some options though, as outlined by the IRS. These include setting up a payment plan or even appealing the garnishment itself through the Collection Appeals Program. In any instance, one should try and avoid a garnishment if at all possible. I mean, once the IRS is getting the money it is owed, do you really think they are motivated to stop the garnishment?

How the tax resolution process works

Tax resolution includes many services and goes by

different names (IRS representation, tax relief, tax problem recovery, tax resolution, tax controversy). However, in summary, tax resolution is a service in which a representative helps a client resolve his or her open debt with the IRS in a way that minimizes the debt as much as possible. The IRS will allow a taxpayer to negotiate a resolution on their own, or the taxpayer can hire a representative to do it on his or her behalf. From a practitioner standpoint, the industry is made up of some major players as well as numerous smaller regional and local firms and practitioners. However, the most important thing to remember is that there are only three types of professionals that can represent you. Those are a CPA, an attorney, or an IRS Enrolled Agent (EA). If the person you are talking to about helping solve your issue does not have one of those designations, they are more than likely a sales associate.

So, once a taxpayer has engaged a professional to represent them, what exactly happens next? It is best to think of tax resolution as a process that is very similar to applying for a mortgage loan. In essence, you are applying for a government loan to pay back some or all of your tax debt. Likewise, you will need to provide much of the same financial information to the representative as you would to a bank. So, while there can be many different steps that are involved based on the amount and type of tax owed, those outlined below tend to serve as the foundation:

- *File IRS power of attorney* – After being engaged, the first thing your representative will do with the IRS is reach out to them and file IRS Form 2848, *Power of Attorney and Declaration of Representative*. This is the form used to authorize an individual (i.e. CPA, attorney or EA) to represent you before the IRS. It effectively tells them that the representative is the person who is handling a taxpayer's situation and that the IRS should deal with that person directly, and not the taxpayer. What is nice about this is that under most circumstances, the taxpayer will not have to interact with the IRS from that point onward. It also gives the representative complete authority and authorization to negotiate a resolution option on behalf of the taxpayer.

- **Obtain and analyze IRS transcripts** – The next phase typically involves the representative reviewing and analyzing a taxpayer's account. This will include:
  o Verifying the validity of the tax debt itself.
  o Determining where a taxpayer sits within the IRS collections cycle, so that it can be broken.
  o Determining what tax returns need to be prepared.
  o Separating out the amount of the debt that is attributable to tax, penalties, and interest.
  o Identifying any opportunities for filing appeals.
- **File all missing tax returns** – This step is the first and most important "actionable" one within the entire process. Why? Well, before the IRS will even enter into a resolution option with the taxpayer, they must be what is referred to as "current and compliant." This means that all their tax returns are filed and that they are making payments toward current obligations (e.g. payroll taxes, quarterly estimated payments, etc). The last thing the IRS will do is accept a resolution option when a person has not solved what got them into trouble in the first place. However, through the transcript analysis performed in the preceding step, the representative should know exactly what returns are outstanding. They will even have most of their source documents if the taxpayer has lost them!
- **Prepare the taxpayer's financial package** – As previously mentioned, the tax resolution process is very similar to that of a loan application. A taxpayer (or their representative) will then prepare IRS Form 433, *Collection Information Statement* which documents things such as income, expenses, assets, and liabilities. Note that there are several variations of this form and the one to be completed will depend on the amount of tax owed and what type of collection representative is handling the case. However, in

the end, the form will yield a number known as the Reasonable Collection Potential (RCP).

- *Apply for and negotiate best resolution option* – The RCP generated in the step above essentially tells the IRS what they can expect to get from a taxpayer. It is a measure of the taxpayer's monthly income less their "allowable" expenses as well as the collection value of the taxpayer's assets. This number will also tell the representative what resolution option(s) are available to the taxpayer. This will be discussed in the next section. Once determined, the representative will work with taxpayers to settle on the one that works for their situation. They will then submit it to the IRS on their behalf so that the case/situation can be closed out.

Author's note: The steps previously presented are a very succinct and high-level overview of the entire process. I purposely did this as each person's situation is entirely unique to them and there can be numerous sub-tracts that need to be administered and navigated. Yet, when boiled down to its simplest form, the above reflects what tax resolution truly is; a form-driven formulaic process. Sure, there are things that need to be considered, the application of various laws and even planning and strategy. However, it is imperative to understand that the process is not simply some "negotiation" between the taxpayer and the IRS.

You see, sometimes due to advertising, people will visit me and have the wrong impression regarding how their situation can be addressed. For example, the Offer in Compromise program is probably the most commonly known tax resolution strategy. This is what you hear about in TV commercials and radio ads, particularly when they talk about settling your tax debt for "pennies on the dollar" (a phrase which the IRS has technically banned advertisers from using). However, it is important to keep in mind that not everybody even qualifies for an Offer in Compromise. Furthermore, this is only one of the many options that might be available to a taxpayer.

So, when someone comes to my office and states that they want an Offer in Compromise, I have to temper their insistence and educate them. I tell them that each option must be explored in relation to the specific facts and circumstances surrounding their tax problem and then the best option can be selected and implemented. In some instances, it may be necessary to employ two or more options to settle their tax obligations. Keep in mind that the ultimate goal is to solve the person's tax problem permanently and for the lowest amount allowed by law.

Tax resolution options - how to solve the issue

So now that you know what the process looks like, how about we discuss the specific resolution options, shall we? When one is trying to resolve a tax matter with the IRS, they have a number of different options at their disposal. Depending on a person's financial circumstances, the amount of their IRS back tax liability and other issues, the options available to them can and will change. However, the following ten specific possibilities are commonly employed to resolve a tax collection matter:

- *Fully pay the tax owed* – While seldom a popular option, sometimes the taxpayer does have the ability to pay the tax outright or borrow against an existing asset (e.g. refinance a home mortgage or take out a home equity loan). Surprisingly, this option is usually the least costly of viable options available to the taxpayer.
- *Filing unfiled tax returns and replacing Substitute for Returns* – When resolving a tax problem, it is relatively common to find that the taxpayer has back tax returns which have not been filed. It is important to note that a settlement cannot be negotiated with the IRS until the taxpayer has filed all outstanding tax returns. Furthermore,

filing unfiled returns to replace "Substitute for Returns" may lower the tax liability owed and the associated interest and penalties.

- **Dispute the tax on technical grounds** – If there is a technical basis to dispute the amount of tax owed, there are a number of paths to consider. These include filing an amended return if the statute of limitations to file has not expired or filing an Offer in Compromise (Doubt as to Liability).

- **Currently Not Collectible Status** – If a taxpayer does not have positive cash flow above the level to pay their necessary living expenses or have equity in assets to liquidate, the taxpayer may qualify for this status. This is most seen when the taxpayer is unemployed or underemployed. In this situation, the IRS places a temporary hold on the collection of the tax owed until the taxpayer's financial situation improves.

- **Installment agreements** – In most cases, the IRS will accept some type of payment arrangement for past due taxes. In order to qualify for a payment plan, the taxpayer must meet a certain set of criteria.

- **Offer in Compromise** – The IRS Offer in Compromise program provides taxpayers that owe the IRS more than they could ever afford to repay, the opportunity to pay a small amount as a full and final settlement. An Offer in Compromise, filed based on the taxpayer's inability to pay the IRS, looks at the taxpayer's current financial position and considers the taxpayer's ability to pay as well as the taxpayer's equity in assets. Based on these factors, an offer amount is determined.

- **Penalty Abatement** – In most cases, penalties make up 10 to 30 percent of the total tax obligation. A penalty abatement request can eliminate some or all penalties if the taxpayer has reasonable cause for not paying the tax on time or paying the appropriate amount of tax.

- **Discharging Taxes in Bankruptcy** – Bankruptcy can

discharge federal income taxes if certain requirements are met. However, this depends upon both the type of bankruptcy and the type of tax owed.

- **Innocent Spouse relief** – Sometimes taxpayers will find themselves in trouble with the IRS because of their spouse's or ex-spouse's actions. The IRS realizes that these situations do in fact occur. In order to help taxpayers that have tax problems which are due to the actions of their spouse, the IRS has developed guidelines for taxpayers to qualify as an innocent spouse. If a taxpayer can prove they meet these guidelines, then the innocent taxpayer may not have to pay some or all the taxes caused by their spouse or ex-spouse.

- **Expiration of the Collection Statute** – The IRS has 10 years from the date of assessment (usually close to the filing date) to collect all taxes, penalties, and interest from the taxpayer. The taxpayer does not owe the tax after the 10-year date has passed.

If you find yourself or a client dealing with a tax balance that you cannot fully pay, just know that there are several options to address with it. The one thing that is not advised is to try and ignore it. I often tell tax debt clients that the IRS is always willing to work with a taxpayer who has a balance. However, they tend to become kind of ornery when you ignore them. Given that the IRS is the most powerful debt collector in the U.S., it is usually not wise to take that approach to resolving a tax matter!

Dealing with an audit

If you do not have problems related to tax debt, that is a good thing. However, I wanted to cover this last topic as everyone stands an equal chance of hitting the audit lottery! Every taxpayer dreads when they receive an envelope with those three bold words on it; Internal Revenue Service. The situation gets worse when you find out that you have been selected for "examination" as the service likes to term it (i.e.

audit). For example, there were 150 million individual tax returns filed for TY 2017, of which 892 thousand were selected for review in FY 2018. Thus, the effective audit rate was 0.6 percent.[3] So, the odds are pretty low that a return will be picked for review. Yet if a person is selected, here are some things to be aware of:

- **Read and follow the directions in the notice.** The audit notice will give you specific information as to what items are being examined. Knowing what is being scrutinized will help you determine what you need to bring to the audit, so you can prove the items in question.
- **Be aware of the response deadlines.** Generally speaking, you only have 30 days to respond to an audit notice. If you do not respond, the IRS can take action, such as automatically adjusting the tax liability. As such, make sure to keep all deadlines top of mind.
- **Organize your records.** Making an auditor's job easier will make the process go all that smoother. The auditor should at least believe that a person is organized and that all of their items are documented and justified. Do not be afraid to group the items in question or attach an Excel summary listing individual amounts that match the tax return. This will allow the auditor to quickly review the important issues. Oh yeah, and do not forget that most auditors like to see receipts, but they are not interested in a garbage bag of them being dropped off on their desks!
- **Replace missing records.** If one goes through their records and finds that some of them are missing, it is best to try and obtain duplicates. Do not just go to the audit and claim that the records are missing or lost. That will not do a person any good at all. At best, the auditor will request that they obtain the records. At worst, the deduction in question will be denied, since there are no supporting documents.
- **Bring only what you are asked for.** I cannot tell you how many people I have seen open themselves up to additional

scrutiny by providing MORE than what was requested in an audit. Leave all additional records and items not requested in the original audit notice at home. That way, if the auditor is curious about something else on the tax return, but the item was not on the original audit notice, you can politely tell him or her that those records are at home. It is likely that the issue will be dropped right there.

- **Do not be a jerk!** While the examiner involved probably does not have any interest in your situation personally, that will probably change if a person acts in a rude or condescending way. Remember, all employees at the IRS are people too. Taking out your frustrations or verbally insulting an auditor will get you nowhere. Also, bear in mind that these people are just trying to do their jobs. So, be courteous at all times, even if the auditor is not courteous or seems unreasonable. If a person arrives at the audit with a large chip on their shoulder, they might make the auditor less willing to see things their way.

- **Only provide copies of documents.** Do not bring original documents to an audit. If you do bring originals, do not give them to the agent. Request that the agent make copies and give the originals back to you. Once you hand over your original documents, there is a very good chance that they will be misplaced or lost. Then you are the one left holding the bag, since the IRS is not responsible for documents lost in its possession.

- **Stay on task.** Auditors are trained to uncover valuable information in what seems to be a simple and friendly discussion. Asking about an expensive new car that a taxpayer might have purchased or that vacation to Barbados might give the auditor reason to believe that they are not reporting all of their income and thus expand the scope of the exam. When meeting with the auditor, you are in essence providing testimony. So, answer as many questions as possible with a simple "yes" or "no" response like one would if they were in court. If you must expound or explain, keep it brief and very much to the point.

- **Know your rights as a taxpayer.** Remember that an audit is like a small trial and it is adversarial in nature. So while one can disagree without being disagreeable, they must know their rights, the audit process, and the law behind the deductions they are claiming. Settling any difference at the audit level is generally best, but if an agreement cannot be reached, know that the battle might have been lost but the war is not over. Everyone has rights that allow them to request a conference with the IRS Appeals Division if an exam does not go their way.

Author's note: Be aware that appeals officers are even more senior than agents with much more experience and knowledge behind them. If one is making an argument that the tax law does not support, the appeals officer will quickly deny it. However, if the issue is complicated and the argument is grounded in tax law and court cases, the appeals officer can make quick work of the analysis – and might just find in a taxpayer's favor. The goal of appeals is to analyze the hazards of litigation and then make a determination on whether they think the IRS has a high probability of winning if it has to go to court. So, if you think your case is truly defensible and the agent was not being reasonable, consider taking it to appeals.

SUMMARY
- The IRS is the revenue service of the U.S. government and is a bureau of the Department of the Treasury. Basically, the IRS is the debt collector and the Treasury is the bank!
- A key difference in the U.S. tax system when compared to other countries is that it is largely one of voluntary compliance. Meaning, it is up to the taxpayer to tell the government how much they earned and should be taxed as opposed to the other way around.
- The IRS has a few tools in its arsenal to get a person to comply with paying the taxes they owe.
- A lien gives the IRS claim to your property. It is their

security towards ensuring that you pay the taxes owed to them.

- A levy is the legal seizure of your property to satisfy a tax debt.

- Tax resolution is a service in which a representative helps a client resolve their open debt with the IRS in a way that minimizes the debt as much as possible.

- While there can be many different steps that are involved in the tax resolution process, those outlined below tend to serve as the foundation:
  o File an IRS power of attorney
  o Obtain and analyze IRS transcripts
  o File all missing tax returns
  o Prepare the taxpayer's financial package
  o Apply for and negotiate the best resolution option

- When you are trying to resolve tax matters with the IRS, you have a number of different options at your disposal. However, ten specific possibilities are commonly employed to resolve a tax collection matter:
  o Fully pay the tax owed
  o Filing unfiled tax returns and replacing Substitute for Returns
  o Dispute the tax on technical grounds
  o Currently Not Collectible Status
  o Installment agreements
  o Offer in Compromise
  o Penalty Abatement
  o Discharging Taxes in Bankruptcy
  o Innocent Spouse relief
  o Expiration of the Collection Statute

- The effective audit rate was 0.6 percent in FY 18, so the odds are pretty low that your return will be picked for review.

- Yet, if it is selected, you should:
  o Read and follow the directions in the notice
  o Be aware of the response deadlines

- o Organize your records
- o Replace missing records
- o Bring only what you are asked for
- o Do not be a jerk
- o Only provide copies of documents
- o Stay on task
- o Know your rights as a taxpayer.

NOTES

[1] Department of the Treasury, Internal Revenue Service, *Data Book, 2018,* Publication 55B, (Washington, DC: 2019), https://www.irs.gov/pub/irs-pdf/p55b.pdf. (Accessed December 24, 2019).

[2] Ibid.

[3] Ibid.

CHAPTER 10
Solving Your Clients Tax Problems
So the Deal Can Close

Sometimes you will get a prospective client who wants to buy a piece of property. During the process of getting all their ducks in a row, it is discovered that the person has a tax problem. Maybe they have not filed their returns in a while. Maybe they have back tax debt or a lien on their credit report. Heaven forbid you are working with a seller to close a deal and the title search reveals that the person has an IRS lien on his or her house. Just how do you get these deals to close? The answer, as you are certain to know by now, is that it depends.

Each scenario listed above can require different actions to solve it. In this chapter, we will look at some of the ways that a broker can help facilitate addressing various tax matters. It is key to know that you do not have to do any of these actions yourself. Nor should you; that should be the job of a qualified and trusted professional within your network! However, knowing what the options are can aid you in getting the deal to the closing table, which is the goal so that you can get paid.

Filing unfiled returns to become lendable

Did you know that per statistics in the 2018 IRS Data Book, there were about *14 million* delinquent taxpayers at the end of 2017 and 2018?[1] That means that the IRS has identified 14 million people who should have filed tax returns but did not. With that said, falling behind on filing one's taxes is something that happens to many people. If you are working with a prospect and it is discovered that they have unfiled returns, your initial thought may be that they are not worth wasting your time on. Yet, I urge you to temper those thoughts. By helping them perform a few steps, they could very easily be put themselves in a position where they are then lendable.

Gather records.

When a person has old tax returns to file, it is important for them to be as accurate as possible. So, the first thing to be done is to pull together all of the original records for the years that were not filed. This may include 1099s or W2's received for work performed, mortgage interest that was paid, or interest, dividends and stock sales. Do not worry if records are missing because the next step will address this.

Secure IRS transcripts.

The original records are supplemented by securing the IRS transcripts that will show what has been reported to the IRS. Basically, one wants to make sure they report everything the IRS has for their SSN, otherwise, they will send the person some notices claiming that they under reported income. Getting the transcripts will cross-check the original records, filling in anything that is missing. The appropriate transcript to request is called the *Wage and Income Transcript*. It can be obtained via the IRS website and can be requested online or by completing IRS Form 4506-T and mailing it in.

Review the past six years of activity.

If the person has six or more years of unfiled returns, make sure that the above two steps are performed for each year. Why? In most cases, the IRS requires the last six years' tax returns to be filed as an indicator of being current and compliant.[2] As such, make this the starting point of the person's analysis. If the person has refunds, they should actually receive them for the last three years' returns UNLESS amounts are owed for other years. In that scenario, the refunds will be applied to any balances due for the other years and any remaining excess will then be refunded to the taxpayer.

Review other sources of income.

The IRS transcripts are a checking point, but you will also need to check for things that are not reported on them. For example, if there is income that was earned that is not on the transcripts (e.g. cash payments), you need to make sure you calculate it and include it on the return.

Review business income and expenses if self-employed.

Income can be recalculated using several methods, including 1099 reporting to the IRS or a person's bank deposits. Working with the income number, determining what was spent to generate that income. When done, take a look at what is left (i.e. the profit). One can then compare that number to what they spent for that year to live (e.g. rent, mortgage, utilities, etc.) to make sure it appears reasonable/logical. Too often, I see tax returns where there is no business profit, which then begs us to ask, "so just how did you live that year?" Rest assured, if I can think of that question, the IRS WILL also be thinking of it too!

Consider filing the returns separately if married.

If the person is married, but only one spouse was responsible for creating IRS debt, strong consideration should be given to filing a separate return. Filing separately can limit who the IRS can collect from – protecting the non-liable spouse.

File original returns and replace any IRS created returns.

Once the entire analysis has been done, the person is ready to file the returns. They can do so on their own or find a qualified tax professional to assist. For example, since I deal with unfiled taxpayers on a frequent basis, I maintain software to file as far back as 10 years. Not only that, but I also maintain all of the tax law for each year so I know how certain things should be treated on that particular year's tax return. If the person decides to tackle it themselves, they will need to obtain the appropriate years' tax forms from the IRS website, complete them manually and mail them in for processing.

As mentioned before, sometimes, when a person does not file a return, the IRS files one for them called a Substitute for

Return (SFR). My experience has been that a SFR is the worst tax return ever! It reports the income that shows up on W2s and 1099s but does not give any deductions or exemptions (which existed prior to TY 2018 under the old law). As such, a prospect may already have a bill from the IRS that was created in connection with a SFR. The good news is that those returns can be corrected, and possibly lower the associated tax and penalties, by filing an "original" return.

File your returns in person if possible.

If the person is doing their returns on their own, the unfiled returns should be hand-filed at an IRS Taxpayer Assistance Center if possible. Note that the centers are by appointment only so do not just randomly visit one as you will be turned away. If you bring an extra copy to the center, you can get it stamped by the IRS as proof of filing. If you are working with an IRS Revenue Officer, the returns should be filed directly with that person. It can take the IRS several months to process the returns. But if you file them directly with their personnel, it can speed up the processing time, which will then "stop the clock" in terms of certain penalties.

Once the returns have been filed and proof of submission generated, your client now has what they need to take to a loan officer. As you can see, the entire process can take a few weeks on the short side and over a month if it is really involved. Thus, it is probably a good idea to always ask a prospective client if they have filed all their tax returns early in the qualification process. If not, you can then direct them on how to get them completed or how to seek out a qualified tax professional. The sooner this is done, the quicker they can begin to work with a loan officer.

Understanding tax lien subordination, withdrawal, and release

When a person owes back taxes, the IRS will generally file a Notice of Federal Tax Lien against them. Tax liens are a matter of public record and available for anyone to look up.

They are typically filed for any balance due that exceeds $10,000. However, new tax liens are usually filed for less than that amount if a person continues to pile on additional tax debt in the future.

The important aspect of a Federal tax lien is that it covers ALL of a person's property. For example, the mortgage on a house is usually only secured by the house itself. But when it comes to a tax lien, it is actually "secured" by everything a person owns. This includes the clothes on their back, the money in their checking account, their retirement accounts, and even their paycheck. A Federal tax lien also shows up on your credit report. This can make it difficult for a person to obtain a bank loan and it will definitely make it hard for a person to sell their home. Yet, there are some ways to deal with a tax lien so that it does not interfere with either situation.

Lien Withdrawal

In extremely rare circumstances, it may be possible to obtain the complete removal of a Federal tax lien. When the IRS withdraws a lien, the lien is erased as though it never existed. This outcome is ideal for your client because it restores their rights to their property, as well as revives their credit score to pre-lien status. In order to achieve this, the taxpayer (or their hired professional) must demonstrate two things:

- The lien is creating an undue economic hardship upon the taxpayer.
- Removing the lien will help facilitate collection of the tax debt.

Basically, you have to show the IRS that the pure existence of the lien will cause a dramatic loss of income. For a business, a lien may interrupt a factoring agreement or a line of credit, which is required for them to operate. For an individual, the existence of a lien might mean the loss of a security clearance, and therefore loss of a job.

Typically, if a person can prove the first bullet, they can often prove the second. For example, if a business continues to operate, and you get to keep your job, then you both can make payments to the IRS, which is what is meant by "facilitate collection."

Lien Subordination

Another tactic that you can sometimes take is to keep the IRS tax lien in place but subordinate the government lien to some other lien. When I do this for a client, I essentially get the IRS to place themselves in second priority position underneath somebody else. The most common reason for doing this is to place the IRS lien secondary to a bank financing lien, such as a factoring agreement, line of credit, or an operating capital loan. Many banks will cut off funding on a loan or line of credit if they are not in first position. Thus, subordinating the tax lien keeps the bank happy by keeping their lien in first priority over the IRS. This keeps a business operating and thereby "facilitates collection."

Lien Discharge

It is not uncommon for somebody to have one particular asset that is worth a bit of money. Sometimes selling that asset, such as a house, can bring in enough money to help pay down a tax debt. Additionally, selling the asset eliminates the associated monthly payment, thereby allowing a person to redirect that money towards their IRS bill each month. See how this all keeps coming back to that "facilitating collection" point mentioned above?

Let us say one of your clients wants to sell their home. It is worth $515,000, but they still owe the bank $400,000 on it. Additionally, they owe back taxes of $150,000 and the IRS has previously filed a tax lien against the taxpayer. So, not only does the bank have a lien on the home, the IRS lien covers it as well. Yet, it is the IRS tax lien that prevents him or her from selling it without the IRS being paid first. Thus, the tax lien needs to be removed by the IRS in order for the home sale to close. The process of removing the IRS lien from this one piece of property is called a lien discharge, and your client must obtain a Certificate of Discharge releasing this one asset only from the lien.

To obtain the Certificate of Discharge, the taxpayer must file IRS Form 14135, *Application for Certificate of Discharge of Property from Federal Tax Lien* with the IRS. The entire process to obtain the certificate (and instructions on how the title company or escrow agent needs to remit funds to the IRS) can take up to 45 days. Thus, you want to engage a tax professional experienced in obtaining tax lien discharges <u>as soon as the client has an offer from a buyer</u>. This will help ensure that closing happens as scheduled and on time.

With the Certificate of Discharge in hand, the prospect can sell their home. This, in turn, allows him or her to pay off the loan without the IRS making a stink about that $400,000 going to the bank. Furthermore, the taxpayer then has $115,000 profit from the sale (less closing and settlement costs) that they can give to the IRS to pay against their $150,000 tax debt. While the client might not be happy about forking that money over to the IRS, at least they get to sell their home and knock down their tax debt at the same time. Plus, you get to earn your commission, so it is a winning situation for everyone!

Author's note: All things lien-related require you to interact with the IRS' Collection Advisory Group. This includes the issuance of all lien-related documents, recording notices with state/local agencies, and providing payoff amounts to stakeholders (e.g. title companies). To that end, if your client has a lien-related matter, it is imperative that you work with a tax professional who knows exactly what to do. As such, it is a good idea to build a relationship with one as early as possible in your career. You never know when a deal might require their assistance to ensure it closes!

SUMMARY

- Filing unfiled tax returns or requesting the IRS to take certain actions regarding a tax lien are some ways to get prospects lendable so they can purchase a home or allow a seller to dispose of theirs.

- If a prospect has unfiled tax returns, the following are the steps they can take so they can become lendable in the eyes of a loan officer:
  o Gather records
  o Secure IRS transcripts
  o Review the past six years of activity
  o Review other sources of income
  o Review business income and expenses if self-employed
  o Consider filing the returns separately if married
  o File original returns and replace any IRS created returns
  o File your returns in person, if possible

- A Federal tax lien can make it difficult for a person to obtain a bank loan, and it will make it hard for a person to sell his or her home.

- Lien withdrawal, subordination, or discharge might be options to allow a client who is trying to sell a property that is encumbered with an IRS lien to actually dispose of it.

NOTES

[1] Department of the Treasury, Internal Revenue Service, *Data Book, 2018*, Publication 55B, (Washington, DC: 2019), https://www.irs.gov/pub/irs-pdf/p55b.pdf (Accessed December 24, 2019).

[2] Per Policy Statement 5-133 and Internal Revenue Manual 4.12.1.3.

CLOSING THOUGHTS

I tried to make the information in this book as easy to follow as possible. However, I do understand that some people may not want to tackle their tax problems on their own. Additionally, some brokers may have reached the point where they don't have the time or desire to undertake their own bookkeeping or taxes anymore. If you find yourself in either situation, then feel free to reach out to us. I have included my contact information at the bottom of this page.

Whether you are a new broker, or one who has been in the industry for some time, it is my sincere hope that you were able to take something valuable away from this book. If it is just one nugget of wisdom or a tactic that you can implement immediately to help grow your business, then my job is done. I know that many readers have probably already started planning out some steps to implement several items from this book! Yet the true key to success is to take action. Remember, determination alone yields nothing unless accompanied with action.

To your continued financial success ---

-- Jared R. Rogers, CPA

Wilson Rogers & Company, Inc
2055 W. 95th St
Chicago, IL 60643

773-239-8850
www.wilsonrogers.net
customerassistance@wilsonrogers.net

INDEX

ABOUT THE AUTHOR

Jared R. Rogers is an Illinois-licensed Certified Public Accountant and CEO of the Chicago-based financial services firm Wilson Rogers & Company. Prior to his current role, he spent 13 years in the finance function of several major companies including Hyatt Hotels, PepsiCo, Robert Bosch, and KPMG LLP. In addition to the above, Jared is also the published author of two other books; *Pathways to Wealth - A Common Sense Guide to Personal Money Management & Lifestyle Techniques* (Authorhouse 2003) and *How to Slash Your Taxes Legally & Ethically* (CreateSpace Independent Publishing 2018).

In his role at Wilson Rogers & Company, Jared is responsible for advising clients on matters including income taxes, tax debt resolution, and personal financial planning. Through his business dealings over the years, he has reviewed thousands of personal and business income tax returns to ensure not only their accuracy, but that the taxpayer is paying the minimal amount of tax that they are legally obligated to.

Philanthropically, Jared has served as Financial Secretary and Treasurer for the IDeaL Education Foundation. He also has previously volunteered as a tax preparer for the IRS' Volunteer Income Tax Assistance Program (VITA), which offers free tax help to low- to moderate-income people who cannot prepare their own tax returns. Over the years, Jared has blogged about numerous tax matters, many of which can be found at www.wilsonrogers.net.

Made in the USA
Columbia, SC
21 December 2020